20/20 Visions
An Invitation to Secret Places in God

By Tom and Marcia Mawman
http://PropheticEquippers.com/

*Forewords by Dr. Sandie Freed, Keith Miller,
and Jeff Wittmer*

20/20 Visions

An Invitation to Secret Places in God

By Tom and Marcia Mawman

http://PropheticEquippers.com/

Forewords by Dr. Sandie Freed, Keith Miller, and Jeff Wittmer

Scripture quotations are taken from the Holy Bible written in the following versions:

The Passion Translation (TPT), Passion and Fire Ministries, Broadstreet Publishing, 2018. All rights reserved.

New International Version (NIV), International Bible Society, Zondervan Publishing, 1973, 1978, 1984.

New American Standard Bible (NASB), Lockman Foundation, 1995.

New Heart English Bible (NHEB), Biblehub.com.

English Standard Version (ESV), Biblehub.com.

Bible Gateway, variety of online versions, Harper Collins Christian Publishing, BibleGateway.com

Bibliography:

King, Patricia, *Eyes that See,* Christian Services Association, 2011.

Freed, Sandie, January 15, 2019 prophetic word, The Elijah List, ww.elijahlist.com, Lifegate Church International.

Miller, Keith, *Eyes to See the Solutions of Tomorrow*, Stand Firm World Ministries Publishing, www.sfwm.org

Wittmer, Jeff, teaching notes from Life Coach training, California Coaching Collaborative Ministries, 2018; www.burningbushlifecoaching.com

DEDICATION

This book is dedicated to our most amazing grown-up children, Jeremiah and Bethany. You inspire us to go for more because you don't settle for mediocrity. We want our ceiling to be your floor in every area of life. We love you more than words can say, and we pray that the encounters we are being blessed to have would be multiplied sevenfold in your lives; then sevenfold in your children, and so on. Our desire is that you may know His passionate love for you more deeply and strongly every day.

TABLE OF CONTENTS

FOREWORD BY DR. SANDIE FREED   1

FOREWORD BY KEITH MILLER   3

FOREWORD BY JEFF WITTMER   4

INTRODUCTION   5

CHAPTER 1:   GODLY IMAGINATION   12

CHAPTER 2:   AN UNEXPECTED VISION   15

CHAPTER 3:   A RETURN TO THE FOREST   18

CHAPTER 4:   THE MUSIC CONDUCTOR   22

CHATPER 5:   CAN I JUMP THAT?   27

CHAPTER 6:   RESTAURANT ON A HILL – THE DREAM   30

CHAPTER 7:   RESTAURANT ON A HILL – THE RETURN   32

CHAPTER 8:   RESTAURANT ON A HILL – THE PROMOTION   37

CHAPTER 9:   THE LIBRARY   40

CHAPTER 10: THE GREAT FALLS   45

CHAPTER 11: THE TELESCOPE ON THE BALCONY   49

TABLE OF CONTENTS

CHAPTER 12: WAY ABOVE THE TREE LINE   52

CHAPTER 13: CASTLE OF THE ANGELS   57

CHAPTER 14: PLAYTIME WITH PAPA   63

CHAPTER 15: GARDEN PORTAL   66

CHAPTER 16: THE WAR ROOM   70

CHATPER 17: THE HALL OF MANTLES   74

CHAPTER 18: PROPHETIC ARTISAN   80

INTRODUCTION TO PART 2   84

CHAPTER 19: PLUNGE IN   90

CHAPTER 20: THE FLYING CARPET   94

CHAPTER 21: FOLLOWING THE LEADER   97

CHAPTER 22: NARROW PASSAGEWAY   100

CHAPTER 23: GREENHOUSE   103

CHAPTER 24: EXPANSION OF THE GARDEN   106

CHAPTER 25: I SET A PLACE FOR YOU   111

TABLE OF CONTENTS

CHAPTER 26: LET'S DANCE 115

CHAPTER 27: BOXES 118

CHAPTER 28: THE WINDMILL 121

CHAPTER 29: LIKE A ROCKET 124

CHAPTER 30: THE KITCHEN 126

CHAPTER 31: THE CLIMB 128

CHAPTER 32: THE CRYSTAL HEART 131

CHAPTER 33: ANGELS TO THE RESCUE 134

CHAPTER 34: THE BRANDING 140

CHAPTER 35: THE BUBBLE 143

CHAPTER 36: A NEW INTERCESSION 147

CHAPTER 37: IN HIS IMAGE 153

APPENDIX A: ONLINE PROPHETIC SCHOOL OFFER 157

APPENDIX B: IS THAT REALLY IN THE BIBLE? 158

APPENDIX C: FIRST THINGS FIRST 161

ACKNOWLEDGEMENTS

A special thanks to Mickey and Sandie Freed, Lifegate Church International, who were at the forefront of this journey for us. You sowed unselfishly by training and equipping us, igniting a passion for the prophetic word, and believing in us by the direction of the Holy Spirit.

Thanks also to Keith Miller, Stand Firm World Ministries, who stoked those flames of passionate pursuit by providing supernatural encounters and impartations through your power-and-glory ministry.

Henry and Tina Malone, Vision life Ministries, we owe you a great debt of gratitude. You were significant catalysts to our freedom. You and our mutual friends stood by us even in the tough times.

To Jeff and Sheri Wittmer, California Coaching Collaborative, we appreciate so much the life-altering teaching that encouraged us more than we can express to embrace the "brilliant shifts" to abundance-based living.

To Patricia McClead, you are sure to have a lot of jewels in your crown as you have poured out so faithfully for us in prayer. I don't think we really understand how significant that has been. Thank you!

To Karla Dial, our friend and very gifted and prophetic editor. Thanks for your great ideas and encouraging words along the way.

To David and Suzanne Lindsay, you've shown us what sacrificial love looks like in "Jesus with skin on."

To Cameron and Alison Smith for making us feel like we can do anything through your encouragement and by demonstrating such great faith in your own lives.

Special thanks to our Mom, Bea Moore, who has been a unique example of unconditional love, acceptance, generosity and forgiveness. To those generations that have gone before us, sowing seeds of righteousness, faith, and sacrifice that we are not even remotely aware of, thank you. May the Lord give you an important part of your reward through what God is doing in our lives. May our whole family be enraptured by the infinite Love of God.

FOREWORD BY DR. SANDIE FREED

I am so excited that you chose to read this book, *20/20 Visions: Invitation to Experience the Secret Places in God.* I am especially proud of its author, Tom Mawman, who is one of my spiritual sons. When I first met Tom and his lovely wife, Marcia, I quickly discerned, in *both* of them, their hearts were sold out to Jesus. I was teaching in our School of Prophets and they were both in training. They eagerly desired to hear the voice of God and allow Him to use them for His glory. I observed how quickly their giftings in God matured, and I witnessed their multifaceted ministry. Over the years, I've observed their integrity in ministry and compassion for the Body of Christ. Like a proud parent boasting on her kids, I just can't say enough about them both. What a gift they are to the Body of Christ!

You are going to enjoy Tom and Marcia's unique writing style. Pages that describe godly encounters, dreams and visions kept me hungering to experience more and more of them myself. And to my surprise, every chapter has an activation which invites you to experience just that—more godly encounters! Yes! You will be led to experience the presence of the Lord in such unique ways. There is opportunity after opportunity to jump in the River and experience realms of God's glory. As Tom describes it: *This book is designed to help people enlarge their capacity to see into the spiritual world through heavenly inspired visions and dreams.* Let that sink in a bit ... your capacity to see into the Spirit is being enlarged! Expect it!

I have always thought it amazing how God uniquely uses people in ministry. The Body of Christ has much diversity in ministry styles. I can assure you that the heartbeat of this book is all about drawing you closer to God and meeting Him time after time in the Secret Place. He invites you to press past your fears, trust Him with your imagination, and soar to new heights in the Spirit.

It's so worth it all to search for *more of Jesus*! It's worth it to take quiet time with Him. It's worth it to be willing to *go out on a limb and exercise raw faith* to see Him in a different dimension. *20/20 Visions* does just that: it empowers

1

each reader to see with new lenses. Dear reader: are you ready for 20/20 spiritual vision? I know you are, and this book will not disappoint!

I have been in ministry for more than thirty years. Being an ordained prophet myself, I am always asking the Lord to *see* better. But more than simply sharpening my prophetic gift, I've realized that through dreams and visions I can *see* with the eyes of my heart. In this book you'll be challenged to stretch your faith and believe for God to anoint your mind and imagination. I encourage you to take this journey. I so enjoyed doing many of these exercises myself.

Tom states that it takes practice to hear from Heaven ... and that is what this book is all about! You're going to practice—but OH! You'll discover that these are the best "practice times" you have ever experienced. Are you ready? It's time to jump in and enjoy! Pray this prayer with me now:

Father, I want to be completely consumed by You. I want to see You, and I want to know more about You. Ignite a passion in me to pursue more of Your divine presence. Let Your glory fill my life and also empower me as I take this new journey. I submit my mind, my imagination, and my heart to You. Holy Spirit, lead me to the Secret Place, and open my eyes to see Heaven. I want to experience your Presence more each day. I yield myself completely to You and Your divine direction. In the name of Jesus. Amen.

I believe a hunger has just been activated in your heart! Holy Spirit is ready to lead you and empower you to arise! You're not just reading a book about prophetic activation—you're invited to a new level of Presence.

God bless you, Tom and Marcia, with divine health and protection as you endeavor to continue to inspire others and to touch Heaven. May you continue to be empowered and overshadowed by His divine presence as you minister to Christ's people all over the world.

Dr. Sandie Freed, prophetic voice to the Body of Christ, mentor to many, pastor, teacher, and author of several books including *Breaking the Threefold Demonic Cord: Discerning and Defeating Jezebel, Athaliah and Delilah* and *Understanding Your Dreams and Visions: How to Unlock the Meaning of God's Messages* (Chosen Books). She and her apostolic husband, Mickey, travel in ministry and are senior pastors of Lifegate Church, International in Hurst, Texas. https://www.lifegatechurch.org

FOREWORD BY KEITH MILLER

As I read Tom and Marcia Mawman's book *20/20 Visions: An Invitation to Secret Places in God,* I knew this wasn't just an ordinary book on prophetic equipping, but a manual to help you discover how the Lord communicates with you through dreams, visions, and the eyes of the heart.

Tom and Marcia are seasoned prophetic teachers and equippers in the Body of Christ. As a gift from the Lord to the Body, they want to equip you to fully navigate the joy of the supernatural realm and the ability to see in images, stories, dreams, and visions. They highlight many different ways the Lord speaks to us through impressions in visions, images, thoughts, and our sanctified imagination.

As Tom and Marcia share stories from their journey in seeing, it will create confidence in your own prophetic journey with the Lord. This book will help you understand and apply your visions and dreams. It will also establish within you a secure ability in the Lord to have and expect dreams and visions from Him. Tom and Marcia point the way of the call of God and also teach truth from the Scripture in a way that will impact your life.

This book isn't meant to be a quick read, but a study with activation so that you will be equipped to draw from the many different ways the Lord will speak to you.

Keith Miller, a prophetic revivalist, is the Founder of Stand Firm World Ministries. Keith has had several encounters with the Lord that have released a strong prophetic and power anointing, seeing signs, wonders, and healing with regional impact. Keith ministers in the Word and anointing, seeing people equipped, empowered, and released into their destiny. See Keith's website for more information: https://www.sfwm.org

FOREWORD BY JEFF WITTMER

A story is told of two small boys around the turn of the century who had never seen a baseball game when they moved from the country into the city. One day, the boys came upon a tall wooden fence blocking them from this mysterious game. One of them found a knothole through which he viewed the game, concluding that it looked quite boring. He only saw one man, moving back and forth at the sound of the crack of a bat. That man would later be replaced by another man with different-colored socks. "What a stupid game," the boy thought.

But when his friend called to him from a tree around the corner from the knothole. Once invited to view the game from high upon a branch, his point of view changed.

The moral is this: When you change your viewing point, your point of view changes. When we view life from God's perspective, the way we see life begins to change.

Tom is like that boy up in the tree. He calls you to a higher viewing point. Not only are his perceptions of prophetic visioning inspiring, but he also offers very practical tools to help you engage in prophetic discovery. I am so excited to recommend this book by my friends Tom and Marcia Mawman. Your viewing point is about to change!

Jeff Wittmer is an advanced ministry training instructor at Bethel School of Supernatural Ministry in Redding, California, where he lives with his lovely wife, Sheri, and the rest of his crew. Jeff is a catalytic communicator awakening people to raise their spiritual intelligence to live a more abundant and vibrant life. Jeff is also a motivational speaker, a certified life coach, entrepreneur, and trainer of coaches and leaders. He is the founder of Burning Bush Life Coaching (burningbushlifecoaching.com) and California Coaching Collaborative, which certifies life coaches.

4

INTRODUCTION

It was a breezy September morning. I guided my blindfolded wife to an open field for her surprise birthday present. "Where are we?" she asked, trying to extract information. I kept silent, enjoying the suspense.

I had secretly arranged for a pilot to meet us for a powered parachute ride. The "aircraft" was nothing more than a cage with a fan behind it and a seat. Long cords trailed behind on the ground, connecting it to a colorful parachute.

The pilot silently waved at me, indicating he was ready. It was time to remove the blindfold. *She is going to be so excited! I thought as I took her* blindfold off.

"I'm NOT going up in that!" my wide-eyed wife exclaimed emphatically.

"What?" I said. "This is your surprise! You always wanted to go up in one of these."

Without missing a beat, Marcia said, "There is no way on God's green earth I am going up in a flimsy cage. I have never piloted anything before."

The disconnect became obvious. She only saw one seat, so she thought she was to fly the aircraft alone. Her fear abated when she realized a skilled, seasoned pilot would be at the helm. She was perfectly safe, with nothing to worry about. Her only job was to sit back and enjoy the peaceful ride.

When these facts became clear, Marcia was able to get in, buckle up and enjoy a thrilling ride into the heavens. Soon she was laughing, taking pictures, and pointing at a beautiful lake down below as she soared high above the ground. It was very comforting to know there was a pilot in charge who was able to bring her back safely.

The same is true for us as we learn to trust God. He is the pilot of our lives and is well able to take us up in the spirit to places He wants us to see.

5

We are eager and excited to go, but only if He navigates, steers, and brings us to His intended destinations. Where He goes, we will follow.

Without exception, we've been created with a desire to experience more of our Creator. He invites us to have supernatural encounters to enhance our knowledge of His great love. He wants to take us on a journey leading to freedom, purpose, and impact.

Keith Miller, a powerful revivalist and founder of Stand Firm World Ministries, states in his book *Eyes to See the Solutions for Tomorrow* (Stand Firm World Ministries Publishing):

> We are living in a new time when every believer needs to function in the ability to see, to have spiritual perception … Spiritual eyesight gives an advantage to Christians to see in the heavenly realm what unbelievers cannot see. We look at the world with our natural eyes, but with our spiritual eyes, we look at the Kingdom of God! Adam and Eve, as eternal spiritual beings, had 20/20 spiritual eyesight in the supernatural realm of the Garden of Eden. They were created for the perfection of that beautiful garden. After their fall through disobedience, they lost their ability to see God and even each other as they had when they were clothed in spiritual light…However, spiritual sight did not completely end for humankind … [in essence, because of God's incredible plan of redemption].

This book is designed to help people enlarge their capacity to see into the spiritual world through heavenly inspired visions and dreams. The entry point for these encounters is always Jesus Christ (John 10:7). He is "the Door," and we enter through Him; there is no other way. Jesus freely provides access to those who are hungry to deepen their relationship with Him.

Christianity is a Spirit-to-spirit relationship. Therefore, we communicate with God through the faculties of our spirit—which mirror our physical senses of sight, hearing, smell, taste, and touch. The primary faculty of our spirit is our ability to see through the eyes of our heart. It follows, then, that the more we refine our ability to see through visions and dreams, the more we encounter the One who is Spirit and lives in eternity.

Jesus modeled this for us. He only did the things He saw His Father doing (John 5:19). He "tuned in" via His spirit, looking for what God was showing Him. Then He spoke accordingly, only speaking about the things He had seen in the presence of His Father (John 8:38). We can follow His example and look for God's pictures in our minds, too.

This book is birthed from a desire to share the experiences Marcia and I have had with the Lord. We sincerely believe God wants to communicate with each of us through dreams, visions, and our sanctified imagination. Before we realize an increase in these areas though, we need to place a high value on what God has to say to us. I admit I have not always valued internal pictures from God. I often discarded them as "silly dreams" or "just my imagination."

I remember getting an interpretation of one of those "silly dreams" once. I was shocked when I learned it contained insightful and critical information that I wished I'd had before I made an impactful life decision. I have since repented and learned to value and earnestly desire God's thoughts and impressions.

The images, stories, dreams, and visions recounted in these pages will provide a new "grid" for seeing into the supernatural realm. The main goal of this pursuit is to grow in intimacy with the Father. Everything revolves around this. No matter where He takes you in the Spirit, no matter what you see, He is the main character, and romance with Him is the plot. The background may change to enhance the plot, but the purpose is to add color and texture to the central love story of our lives.

Can this point be overlooked? Yes; some want the fruit that others have without paying the price of intimacy. They try to find shortcuts through the process and skip the intimacy part. They may want to see more miracles, signs, and wonders, or to increase their ability to see into the heavens. Agreed, those things are wondrous—but if you don't gain intimacy with Him, you've missed the whole point.

NOW THIS IS ETERNAL LIFE: THAT THEY KNOW YOU, THE ONLY TRUE GOD, AND JESUS CHRIST, WHOM YOU HAVE SENT. (JOHN 17:3 NIV)

The undercurrent of this book is to bring you into a greater passion to know Him more. We want to know what He has to say about us, our lives, and how He thinks and feels. We want to know His point of view. Allowing Him to speak to us through visions provides an excellent communication tool to do just that. Remember, the goal is to know Him. The development of your spiritual eyes, therefore, is not something that's just "nice to have"; rather, it is a necessity. It is pivotal to our spiritual growth. God can use a picture to speak volumes. As the saying goes, "a picture is worth a thousand words."

Is it easy to see more from Heaven? No; it takes practice, like anything else. People often compare their prophetic gift with others'. I often tell them, "If you want what they have, do what they did to get it." I like what Pastor Bill Johnson of Bethel Church says when people ask him to pray over them for a "double portion": "If it worked that way, I would lay hands on myself!"

No, we can't take shortcuts. We must practice. I find the following scripture very encouraging because it indicates that our senses can indeed be trained.

SOLID FOOD IS FOR THOSE WHO ARE MATURE, WHO THROUGH TRAINING HAVE THE SKILL TO RECOGNIZE THE DIFFERENCE BETWEEN RIGHT AND WRONG.
(HEBREWS 5:14 NIV)

To foster this training environment, at the end of each story we invite you to develop your own unique, personal encounters with the Lord by completing the activation questions. Simply read a chapter and then journal, seeking God's spontaneous flow of thoughts and pictures.

The encounters found herein reflect intimate, personal times my wife and I have had seeking God. You'll notice He speaks to us differently. My wife's nickname from God is "Love Dove" (mine is not, thankfully). The tone, imagery, and experiences also vary, as do our writing styles. My sections are included first, then Marcia's chapters begin with an introduction midway through the book.

I was reluctant at first to share my personal and intimate experiences with the Lord. For years, my sweet wife would exhort me by saying, "Hon, these are amazing, you should share these in a book. Others would love to read them." I thanked her for the vote of confidence and shrugged off the idea. Then one day, God got my attention. A man I hardly knew walked up to me, looked me in the eye, and said, "God told me to ask you, 'When are you going to start writing?'" Then he walked away, apparently satisfied he had completed his mission.

The message was clear. The Lord's gentle hints given through my wife were ignored, so He turned up the volume. I realized I'd better get busy!

The challenge we all have is to get away and become quiet with the Lord. We are bombarded with things vying for our attention daily. Our phones

8

notify us of what we're missing on Facebook, Instagram, Pinterest, YouTube, WhatsApp, Messenger, etc.; the list goes on. However, the Bible says to "be still and know that I am the Lord" (Psalm 46:10). It's a bit paradoxical, but "stillness" requires work, and it is foreign to us. We have to work at saying "no" to the distractions of our high-tech world and saying "yes" to quieting ourselves. The work has a payoff: it yields the surpassing treasure of knowing Him.

The Bible says as we come to God, we must approach in faith, expecting Him to be present. The same principle applies to dreams and visions. "Without faith, it is impossible to please God" (Hebrews 11:6). If we enter the world of dreams and visions with doubt, we will find it takes us nowhere. But if we approach it as children, eager to play, explore, and imagine, a new world will open up to us. He wants to reveal secrets to us.

... BUT THERE IS A GOD IN HEAVEN WHO REVEALS MYSTERIES. (DANIEL 2:28 NIV)

We also must protect the eye gate, the images we allow to enter. Do we focus on heavenly things or natural things?

SINCE, THEN, YOU HAVE BEEN RAISED WITH CHRIST, SET YOUR HEARTS ON THINGS ABOVE, WHERE CHRIST IS, SEATED AT THE RIGHT HAND OF GOD. SET YOUR MINDS ON THINGS ABOVE, NOT ON EARTHLY THINGS. (COLOSSIANS 3:1 NIV)

If we focus on the brilliance of heavenly images, then those images increase in us, making it easier to see visions. Conversely, if we focus on images of darkness, fear grows, and the desire for those dark things increases; lust and corruption begin to take over, resulting only in bondage. Whatever we focus and present ourselves to gains power in our lives.

*DON'T YOU REALIZE THAT GRACE FREES YOU TO
CHOOSE YOUR OWN MASTER? BUT CHOOSE
CAREFULLY, FOR YOU SURRENDER YOURSELF TO
BECOME A SERVANT—BOUND TO THE ONE YOU
CHOOSE TO OBEY. IF YOU CHOOSE TO LOVE SIN, IT WILL
BECOME YOUR MASTER, AND IT WILL OWN YOU AND
REWARD YOU WITH DEATH. BUT IF YOU CHOOSE TO
LOVE AND OBEY GOD, HE WILL LEAD YOU INTO
PERFECT RIGHTEOUSNESS. (ROMANS 6:16 TPT)*

What about the gray areas? We agree that focusing on darkness has an adverse effect on us, but what about setting our mind on "neutral" and non-sinful things? For example, I love seeing movies. I could spend hours filling my mind with action-packed adventure scenes. One day, I was talking to a friend about the latest movie when he turned the conversation toward spiritual matters.

"Tom, what has God been showing you lately?" he asked. I recoiled from the question and had to stop and think. As he was eating, my friend unknowingly made a comment that pierced my heart.

"Yeah," he added, "I find that entertainment dulls my spiritual senses." Those simple words lingered in my heart, long after my friend left. I do not want my spiritual senses dull. What must I do to keep my attention on God?

Let this book be a catalyst to sharpen your spiritual senses and enhance your ability to see into heavenly realms. The only prerequisite is that you are a Christ-seeker, open for Him to lead and guide you into truth.

In addition to this book, we have also made available an online school that you can attend to further hone your spiritual senses. In it, you learn to hear God better, grow in intimacy with Him, and expand your ability to deliver your prophetic words with increased accuracy. See Appendix A in this book to learn more.

In closing this introduction, I'll leave you with a powerful word from my friend and mentor in the prophetic, Dr. Sandie Freed. The following was published by the Elijah List on January 15, 2019:

I heard the Lord say, "I am calling My children to come up higher. There is revelation being given to those who hear this invitation and act upon it. As My Church draws nearer to Me, I will open doors of understanding and wisdom. As I release more understanding and godly wisdom to My Church, expect increase! Understanding and wisdom will activate the atmosphere for prosperity, inventions, medical breakthroughs, and miracles. I am going to reveal many hidden mysteries concerning dreams and visions in this season."

Chapter 1

GODLY IMAGINATION

One of the greatest gifts God has given mankind is His imagination. This powerful tool enables us to create anything we can visualize. The world's great artists, poets, writers, and leaders of business have achieved that level of success because they used their imagination.

I love what Albert Einstein wrote:

"When I examine myself and my methods of thought, I come close to the conclusion that the gift of imagination has meant more to me than any talent for absorbing absolute knowledge. All great achievements of science must start from intuitive knowledge. I believe in intuition and inspiration ... At times, I feel certain I am right while not knowing the reason."

In the 1950s, author Napoleon Hill wrote, "The imagination is literally the workshop wherein are fashioned all plans created by man."

We recognize that imagination is used to build things—but what about using it to gain spiritual revelation? Often God speaks to us through faint impressions or visions of the mind. Yet we discount these as "just our imagination." If you have ever been belittled for having an active imagination, perhaps it's time to forgive and renew your appreciation for this precious gift. Our imagination was given to us as a receiver to pick up on the signals God transmits to us.

Apostolic minister and prophetic voice Patricia King reveals more of the importance of using our imagination in her excellent book, *Eyes That See* (Christian Services Association, 2011). She writes:

The faint impressions in the mind and imagination are the most common ways that God reveals vision to his people. Often believers feel this is not a significant vision; that it's a lower-level vision than perhaps an open vision. This is not true. There are no lower or higher levels of vision. They are simply different ways He uses to reveal His will and purpose. Each way is precious if God is the source. Most seasoned and credible prophets will confirm that the most predominant way God speaks to them is the still, small, God thoughts in the mind, and the faint impressions of the imagination.

This confirms what we have seen throughout years of teaching a prophetic school. The more some students tap into faint impressions from God and pictures in their imagination, the more others are impacted and testify that they are indeed hearing from God. Whatever we are thankful for and focus on, we get more of. The more we honor and appreciate this revelation, the more it will deliver. The more we practice, the stronger our ability to see will become. (See Hebrew 5:14.)

So, what role does imagination play in creating heavenly doors into the spiritual realm? To answer that question, we first need to make a distinction between "sanctified imagination" and "visions from God." Are the two the same thing? No, of course not! My imagination begins with me. I can choose to use my imagination to picture an elephant. This picture is 100 percent my doing. God's supernatural vision starts with Him and is authored by Him. We never mix these two up and say my vision is a divine vision. We can, however, invite the Holy Spirit to take over a scene in the imagination. When we do, we experience an inner flow which moves with a life of its own. It then becomes His inspired vision; we just capture it by writing it down to review and evaluate later. My godly imagination is mine; God's vision is His.

However, it does require "priming the pump." In years past, I have joked with friends in prophetic ministry that people should not seek to be the first in the line to receive a prophetic word. It may take a while before revelation is abundant.

"Priming the pump" is a term dating back to a time when people had to repeatedly pull down on well handles to draw water up out of the deep cistern. My grandfather knew this process well. He owned a small farm in Illinois and extracted water manually from his well. It required a lot of effort to draw the water up. When I was a boy, I thought I would show how strong I was by quickly drawing water using the heavy iron handle. To my frustration, it took "all day" to draw water (in reality it was probably only eleven cranks, which seemed like forever to a young boy). Once water flowed, however, maintaining the flow was almost effortless, requiring only an occasional crank to keep it going.

Revelation uses the same process. Our imagination acts like the cistern handle. At first, nothing noteworthy happens, and we are tempted to quit. It is sad to think how many people give up only seconds before the flow begins! If we stay with it, however, imagination gives way to a spontaneous flow of the Holy Spirit. In this way, our imagination acts as a catalyst to draw from revelation deep inside. When our "living water" springs up, we collect it through writing.

For further study on the biblical basis for sanctified imaginary, we have added a collection of scriptures in Appendix B.

Chapter 2

AN UNEXPECTED VISION

It was a Monday, six o'clock in the morning. I was praying about the stressful workday ahead while on a business trip in San Antonio, Texas. I was leading an audit of a customer service department, and it was not going well. I began to cry out in prayer for help. Suddenly, a scene appeared in my mind which had a life of its own. It was like watching a movie. I didn't make it happen, nor did I try to stop it. I simply observed.

I found myself in a lush ravine with tall trees. As I looked up, I saw branches swaying with the summer breeze. Leaves were responding to it with an almost musical rustling sound. A babbling brook nearby flowed to an unknown destination. It was about fifteen to twenty feet across and shallow.

After absorbing the sights and sounds of this picturesque scenery, I noticed I had a visitor who walked toward me on the water. His face was cheerful and bathed in soft light. He looked overjoyed to see me; it felt like a reunion with a dear friend.

He grabbed my neck, laughing affectionately, and pulled me close to His chest to hug me. All my questions about being accepted melted away in an instant. Then He put His arms on my shoulders, as guys do when wrestling. I mimicked Him, locking my arms across His. My mind began to assess the situation. *My odds of winning are not very good ...*

Then my eyes connected with His intense, piercing gaze. It's hard to explain the sensation. I felt vulnerable and transparent, yet completely safe and accepted at the same time. He affectionately said with a smile, "I know who you are. You're playful."

Those who know me can attest to the truth of this statement. Playfulness is not the typical trait of an auditor; my secret was out. Yes, I was only playing the auditor role out of obligation, which is contrary to my temperament. With a few words, He revealed it all. The One who knows, truly knows me, was standing in front of me.

With contagious laughter, we began to spin in this wrestlers' shoulder lock. Then unexpectedly, Jesus reached down and splashed me with water! Then He laughed and did it again!

"Oh, it's so on!" I said. The water fight continued until we were both drenched.

He motioned for me to climb a nearby granite rock face. (Rock climbing is a hobby of mine.) We didn't have ropes, but given the company I was in, I wasn't worried. Side by side, we climbed up the nearly 100-foot slab of granite. He suddenly looked at me with a mischievous smile and pushed off into the air. His body did a slow, graceful backflip. After a few seconds of free-falling, He opened a parachute and yelled, "Your turn!"

I pushed off the rock. My descent was not as graceful; my arms were flapping as if that would help slow my fall. To my relief, I noticed I, too, had a parachute. *Where did I get this?* I pulled the cord and followed Jesus safely down to the ground.

It was an exciting, adrenaline-pumping rush. It was just as real as any memory of any vacation I've ever had. (Even now as I am re-telling it, it feels like it just happened.)

My surroundings suddenly changed. My heart was still racing in my chest, I found myself once again sitting in my hotel room in San Antonio in work clothes. The clock revealed that I was now late, but I wasn't ready for reality to set in. I ignored it and continued to think about the experience.

I wonder if I could do it again.

I could hardly wait to try.

IT'S YOUR TURN TO PRACTICE

Use the following activation questions to enhance your prayer time with the Lord. Begin by finding a quiet time and place. Remove any distractions (including smartphones).

Picture yourself in the scene described above. Take your time; there's no rush. What is He highlighting to you? Look for Jesus in the scene. What is He doing? What does He say to you?

Ask the Lord these two-way journaling questions. Take time to listen and write down His response.

1. Lord, what do You love about me?

2. Is it OK to be playful with You?

3. What are things I do that please You and bring You joy?

4. What can I do to have more joy?

5. Show me how I'm fully known by You.

6. Meditate on Mathew 18:2-5: What can I do to be more childlike?

Chapter 3

A RETURN TO THE FOREST

I returned again to the forest I described in the chapter titled "An Unexpected Vision." I was surprised to learn how easy it was. I was delighted I could return to it. I took a moment to allow the epiphany to sink in: when God gives you a vision, you can return to it. The door to that place remains open.

It doesn't take long. I see Jesus waiting for me to join Him. He is standing on the surface of a small river with water flowing around His feet.

He motions for me to join Him on the water. As I do, I am pleased to find it is solid against my weight. I can stand. So I venture out, forgetting that this defies the laws of physics.

As I approach, He greets me, and we begin to walk upstream on top of the water. He says, "I am calling you to travel on unconventional paths, just as walking on water may be unconventional."

The stream in front of us is obstructed by a small, seemingly impassable waterfall. To solve this problem, I reach down to my feet and open a hidden trap door. Water rushes in. I step through it, now soaked, and find a way to tunnel past the obstruction to the level ground. I look at Jesus, proud of my accomplishment.

With a chuckle, Jesus says, "That's one way of doing it. You created a door and walked through it. That was ingenious and a way through the obstacle. You often think outside the box and trust your ingenuity to figure a way out of a jam. However, you did not ask Me for the solution."

Jesus turns as if to demonstrate. He effortlessly walks on top of the obstruction and past it. With His arm now around my shoulder, He says, "If you had asked Me, you would not have had to get wet in a water tunnel, fighting to get to the surface."

18

The admonition is gentle and filled with love. He then changes the tone and tries to get me to laugh by scooping up water in His hand and splashing me in the face with it. Only a few sprinkles land.

I look at Him somberly and say, "In a very respectful way, with sincere admiration and love, I now splash You." I splash Jesus and laugh.

He laughs, too. Returning the favor, He reaches down, fills two hands with water and proceeds to pour them on my head while saying, "Respectively, Tom, I now splash thee."

He must have added something supernatural to it, because the volume of water is not what was cupped in His hands—no, sir! It reminds me of those waterparks that have a 100-gallon bucket slowly filling on top of the highest part of an adventure area for kids. When it is full, it tips over and drenches everyone in its path. That is precisely how this feels. It lasts for about thirty seconds.

Jesus is barely wet. I am beyond soaked but loving every minute of it. I never imagined Jesus to be this much fun.

I try to recover by shaking the water off my hair and face. I now have a super-soaker gun fully loaded. I repeat, "Respectfully and reverently, I now douse You." Then I proceed to nail Jesus with the water gun. This time, I don't miss my target.

He responds by saying, "Oh, you want more?"

It begins to rain over my head. The cone above me turns to heavy rain.

"No fair!" I complain. "You control the weather!"

I use my imagination and picture buckets on a string over His head, each filled with water. I yank on one end hoping for all the buckets to spill water on Him—but the water turns to butterflies that all fly away before one drop lands on His head.

Jesus is cracking up, laughing hysterically.

I concede, "OK, OK, I give up. I surrender, You win." I reach out to give Him a polite concession hug.

As I do, a wave of acceptance floods my soul. It hits me like the water dousing I just experienced; wave after wave of pure acceptance, more than anyone has ever offered.

Tears well up in my eyes as I sway from the effects of the love bomb. I am now drunk with love, barely able to walk. Looking into my eyes, He says, "I deluge you with My love, just like the water in that fight. Not in a small measure, but in abundant submersion. Great is My love for you, Son. I love you! I love everything about you. You are Mine. I fully accept you. You are safe!"

I linger in this beautiful moment, not wanting to leave. Time itself stands still. Somehow, it's healing the wounds from the past; the careless, hurtful words, the rejection, and the self-hatred. All of it dries up in this beautiful, warm place of eternal acceptance.

The vision ends. I am aware of my surroundings now, but forever changed.

IT'S YOUR TURN TO PRACTICE

Picture yourself in the scene described and look for Jesus. Take your time. What is He highlighting to you? What is He doing? What does He say to you?

Ask the Lord these two-way journaling questions. Take time to listen and write down His response.

1. Lord, do I believe I need to earn love and perform for it?

   a. Why do I believe this?

   b. What do You want me to believe?

   c. How is unconditional love different?

2. Lord, are You in a good mood?

3. Lord, show me a revelation of Your love and acceptance.

Chapter 4

THE MUSIC CONDUCTOR

THE HEAVENS DECLARE THE GLORY OF GOD; THE SKIES PROCLAIM THE WORK OF HIS HANDS. (PSALM 19:1 NIV)

The encounter begins with a simple scene from Scripture. Jesus is with His disciples, enjoying conversation around a campfire after a long day of ministry. Jesus then excuses Himself from His friends to spend some time alone to pray. It is a starry night with the Milky Way on full display, shouting the glory of God. Jesus is sitting on a large rock with a flat surface, about ten to fifteen feet across.

At first, I don't want to disturb Him; I just watch patiently from a distance. It is a sight to see, the Creator sitting under His creation. A Man filled with love and compassion, with no pretense, no haughtiness, no ambition other than to win back the lost and perishing. The scene begins to take on a life of its own, like watching a movie; I capture the spontaneous thoughts that follow.

I hear my name, and it almost startles me. I was comfortable observing the scene, but I forgot He could see me. He is now staring at me, motioning for me to sit with Him. I eagerly run across the flat rock to sit next to my friend. He affectionately hugs my shoulder, showering my soul with feelings of safety and peace. I get the sense nothing can harm me; everything is going to be OK.

"Lord, I wonder if Your disciples understood the rare gift they had while sitting next to a campfire under the stars. Did they fully comprehend the Creator of the lights above them was sitting next to them?" I ask.

"Some entertained the thought," He says. "For others, it was too lofty of an idea to fully comprehend." He hands me something. "Here, take a look."

I open my hand, but nothing is in it. Maybe this is a joke. I awkwardly laugh.

"You must take it by faith before you see it," He says.

So, I extend my hand again and imagine taking hold of a telescope. I raise it to my eye. As soon as I do, the sky and the stars are amplified. Formerly small specks of light are replaced with blue and green gas swirls mixed with deep violet and red. It's magnificent!

"Now listen for a moment, turn your music off," He says. (Music has been playing on my phone.) "Just be still."

There is a faint popping noise which has a rhythm to it—a slow, methodical, drum-like beat. There is also a higher-pitched fizzling sound.

"Now let's add them together," He says.

The rhythm of the two is compelling, but it also lacks something. "Should I add more?" He asks.

"Yes, please," I eagerly reply.

He then highlights galaxies and their unique sounds. A masterful orchestra Conductor is in front of me, prompting various instruments to be recognized at the right time. Entire galaxies respond to the summons, bringing their unique music, contributing to this living intergalactic orchestra.

"Bravo!" I applaud. "Bravo!"

He acknowledges my excitement with a smile. Nonchalantly, He continues to add more complex beats, harmonies, and melodies of creation. Without warning, a deep whale sound is added, sounding like a moaning tuba. He enjoys startling me and laughs; I can tell He is having fun.

I then see and hear dolphins giving familiar chirping sounds, like laughter, as they dive gracefully out and back into the water.

Sounds of unusual animals are added: elephants, bison, and other beasts of the field. Then, birdsong is introduced with chirping high notes, along with cranes and loons, all in time with the original beats of galaxies and stars.

"Oh Lord, please promise me when I get to Heaven, You will do this for me again."

"It will be My pleasure. All of creation is under My command, but do you know what moves My heart more than any of these?" He says.

I shrug my shoulders to suggest I don't. Could anything top this? The Creator in His conductor's role, playing heavenly melodies.

Jesus continues, "All the wonders of My creation don't captivate My heart the way My children do; the way you do. Let that sink in a moment. Don't rush past the thought." He pauses for a moment.

Then He continues looking directly at me with affection. "You are the apple of My eye; you are the one My soul desires. You are the one who ravishes My heart. Each and every son and daughter is precious. Their prayers are sweet music to me, more beautiful than any sound found in the cosmos. I have paid the ultimate price to have My bride."

I begin to reflect on the sacrifice He made. "This is possible because Jesus took the rap for me; died my death to pay for my rebellion and sin …

"I can commune with the Master and watch Him orchestrate the galaxies like a conductor. It's beyond comprehension."

Jesus enjoys the thought, too.

FOR THE JOY SET BEFORE HIM, HE ENDURED THE CROSS, SCORNING ITS SHAME, AND SAT DOWN AT THE RIGHT HAND OF THE THRONE OF GOD. (HEBREWS 12:2 NIV)

"I could watch and listen to those sounds for years," I tell Him. My mind then drifts to a prophetic word I received about having no limitations.

Knowing my thoughts, He says, "Like a transplanted plant, you can now grow without limitation. There is no wall or boundary to restrict you. You can expand into whatever your heart desires. What do you want to build? You can go anywhere with Me. You will not have limitations in this rich, fertile soil."

His comments cause me to reflect on the difficulties I have had in past seasons. They are too intricate to mention here, but I did feel like growth was limited and my time was spent with activities not in line with my purpose.

Jesus continues, "Gaze on Me and My glory, and I will expand your borders and help you grow into a beautiful, fruitful vine and shade for My people. A tree never has to strive to be a tree and grow. It just soaks up the rain and sunshine, and its roots automatically go deeper. It receives rays of love and encouragement, edification. Then automatically, it gives fruit. You are fruitful as you abide in Me. Dream, stretch, and play; play and dream, dream and play. The more you are comfortable being like a child around Me, the more refreshed you will be. Refreshment, vision, and joy will return. There are no limits to what you can be in Me or what you can become. Don't

24

rush it. Just enjoy the process and let the fruit come naturally, bursting from the abundance I will expand inside you."

I give Jesus a hug goodbye and say, "Thank you, Jesus, I really appreciate it."

IT'S YOUR TURN TO PRACTICE

Engage your imagination using the story you just read. Encounter Jesus in it. Look carefully at details until you can see more. Ask the Holy Spirit to speak to you through this exchange. Let your dialog flow naturally. What would you like to ask Him?

The following are additional questions. Write down what He tells you.

1. Am I really more important to You than the heavens in all their majesty?

2. What lies have I believed about my importance to You? How can I replace them with truth?

3. What are the ways my growth has been limited? What can I do to move forward?

4. Read Song of Songs 4:9-11 and ask the Lord to speak to you through it.

5. What impact does my worship have on Your heart?

6. What new things are You showing me in the spiritual realm?

Chapter 5

CAN I JUMP THAT?

Using godly imagination, I picture the beautiful forest again. I can hardly wait to meet Jesus.

This visit is already different because there is no sign of Him. I study the scene while I wait. The leaves of nearby aspen trees are bold yellow, reminiscent of an autumn landscape. The swift creek collects the fallen leaves, which refuse to be swept away in spots.

Then I catch a glimpse of the Master walking on the stream. He walks with authority, purpose, and power. *Indeed, this will be a different experience*, I think. He stops and motions for me to follow Him, on top of the water.

I hesitate at this strange invitation. It's almost a casual request, as though the water has no problem supporting my weight. I'm willing, but ... *Just how does someone walk on water?* I muse. I settle on the simple answer, *By faith, of course.*

I take a breath, look at Him, and step up onto the water, trusting I will not sink. It works! He is not surprised at my achievement. Instead, He quickly turns around and walks in the other direction. "Hold on a second!" I protest, now running to catch up.

The scene changes, and I am on a mountaintop. A range of beautiful snow-capped peaks stretches for miles. "Follow Me," Jesus says. He begins to jump from one mountain summit to the next, as though they are stones in a shallow stream a few feet apart.

"You walked on shallow water. Is this any different?" He says without slowing His stride.

"Ah ... yeah it is!" I protest as I leap to the next peak. While I am in the air, the distance folds somehow. I land on the subsequent ridge, hearing laughter from a distant mountain; Jesus is enjoying this. I wonder what fantastic adventures He took his disciples on after hours. (See John 21:25.)

27

I continue to leap and bound between mountaintops, exhilarated by each landing. I am getting the hang of it. The rush of adrenaline causes my heart to pound as I hear encouragement from the Master. "Now you're getting it!" He says.

After a while, the scene changes again. I am now in outer space, standing on top of a planet.

"Don't tell me—more stretching," I say. Without hesitation, Jesus begins to leap across planets and stars as though they are mountains. Casually He says, "Come on, like this." He then leaps into a shaft of light; He and the light disappear, like in a *Star Trek* movie. Then in a flash, He is on a distant planet.

"Your turn!" He yells.

Without thinking, I leap. The shaft of light appears and sucks me into it. I am being pulled by light, stretching without pain. Then within seconds, I am at the next planet; the shaft opens and closes, spitting me out. Planet after planet rushes by until I hear Him say, "I am going to increase your faith for the impossible. I will usher you into a new journey of supernatural faith that will be out of this world. Follow My lead and step into it boldly without doubting. You'll find there are no limits with Me. There are no boundaries I can't cross. I invented the laws of physics. They bend and shift at My command. Nothing is impossible for those who believe."

The scene changes again. I am aware of the chill from the overworked hotel room air conditioner. I am back.

IT'S YOUR TURN TO PRACTICE

Did you catch the fact that I re-entered a previous vision? The door remains open; how exciting! How can we use this revelation to enhance our fellowship with Him? How can we hone our spiritual senses and expect God to encounter us, just like Adam did in the cool of the day (see Genesis 3:8)?

Quiet your mind. Picture yourself in the scene described above. Step into it by faith. Allow the Holy Spirit to take over the scene.

The following are sample questions. Find those you would like to ask the Lord now.

1. What limitations have I put upon You?

2. Lord, what limitations have I put upon myself?

3. What do You want me to stretch my faith toward in this next season?

4. How can I take practical steps to stretch toward the impossible?

5. What risks do You want me to take?

Chapter 6

RESTAURANT ON A HILL – THE DREAM

One night I had a vivid dream in which I was walking up a dirt road on a rocky hill. I saw mountains like the Swiss Alps all around me. The vistas in every direction were beautiful, beyond comprehension.

Sitting on top of the hill, like a crown jewel set in a magnificent setting, was a restaurant with no roof. As odd as it may seem, there was no covering on the building, just open sky. This omission seemed to symbolize peace, vulnerability, and access to an open Heaven.

It was made of marble and had exquisite curved architecture. Everything looked hand-carved. The pillars had stories of battles carved into them. There was a courtyard with polished onyx stones set in a pattern along the floor.

There was sweet-sounding music coming from the courtyard. People were eating, drinking, and generally enjoying themselves. Could this be a restaurant? They wore clothes from the Renaissance era. Their robes, tunics, and big hats were individual expressions with artistic flair. All their countenances were surprisingly radiant; in fact, they were beaming.

I was about to enter the building when I was suddenly yanked back from this glorious place by my alarm clock.

"Really? You have to be kidding me!" I murmured. I was more than a little frustrated. I lay in bed trying in vain to return to my dream. The light of the morning flooded my eyes; the day had begun. The dream lingered in my head as I analyzed it.

I know I have never seen a building like that before ... Was it a building in Heaven?

IT'S YOUR TURN TO PRACTICE

In this activation, it's time to dream again. Ask God for a dream and write it down when you get it. Then work with the Holy Spirit to interpret it. Journal with Him about the insights He gives.

Next, ask Him for a dream of a real heavenly place. Then during your journaling time, ask God to take you on an adventure there. For an example of this, continue reading "Restaurant on a Hill – The Return.

Chapter 7

RESTAURANT ON A HILL – THE RETURN

A short time later, I had the following spontaneous thought: *What if I meet with Jesus at the restaurant in my dream? If the dream was from God, maybe it was an invitation? Could I use my new memory of it as a catalyst to re-engage with it during my journaling time?*

In the movie *The Chronicles of Narnia: Prince Caspian*, the characters return to Narnia through a painting of a ship on the water. Similarly, past spiritual experiences, including open visions, angelic encounters, dreams, and testimonies of miracles are like living pictures hanging on the walls of our mind. If mixed with faith, they become a door or portal to the supernatural.

Using the method just described, I purposed to use my imagination to "retrace my steps" to the restaurant in my dream and share a meal with Jesus. I just did it by faith, and it worked. Let's step into the experience as though it is only now happening.

I approach the courtyard of this surreal place. In the archway, a tall, broad-shouldered young man greets me with a smile and says, "This way please, the Master is waiting."

He escorts me to the back patio. The breathtaking panoramic view of mountains overwhelms me. I pretend not to be awestruck, but my face gives me away. Nearby, there is a short railing with intricate carvings. I sit down at a table arrayed with baked goods. My eyes wander to the nearby scenery. Some of the mountains drip with waterfalls, as if they have sprung a leak. The water does not just spill over the top; it sprays down from the rock pores.

Returning my gaze to this building, I notice something odd. The missing roof shimmers like the top of water catching sunlight. It is translucent. *So strange ... is there more to this place than meets the—?*

A narrow shaft of light appears, interrupting my thoughts. A humble Jewish carpenter steps out of it. The thin thread of light disappears behind Him. Jesus's face is radiant with a soft, peaceful white light. He brings a sense of wellbeing, a sense of being safe, accepted, and loved, all at the same time.

Respectfully, I take a knee with my head bowed. With a smile, He says, "Have a seat, My friend."

There is a smell in the air like a bakery early in the morning. I can detect fresh bread, which wafts through the air like a fine mist.

He hands me a large berry. "Try this."

"Wow, it's sweet, not tart," I reply.

We continue to sample food together, not paying much attention to the passage of time. We enjoy each other's company.

It's hard to explain, but time itself seems to move slower or is suspended when I'm with Him. It feels like we are here for a very long time, even years. It's like we are outside of time. Perhaps this is what it's like being with Someone who inhabits eternity. Selah.

I offer a question. "What are some ways I can learn to live out of Your voice each day?"

"Good question," Jesus says as He sips His drink. "Every movement of your heart toward Me is significant."

I notice holes in His wrists. "Are those holes in Your wrists from my sin?" I ask.

"Yes," He replies, "but let's not talk about that right now."

I change the subject, "Lord, yesterday I saw a woman who looked like she was beaten up pretty bad. It must be difficult for an omnipresent God to see evil every day, continually. I mean, it must be hard to watch."

Jesus gazes away for a moment, then says, "I see the abused and the abuser."

He pauses for a moment before continuing, "I recognize it generationally, too. I see the root of the pain, where it came from, many generations ago. Broken fathers are unknowingly imparting their brokenness to their children. The children then grow up and lash out against their children and so on. Vows and judgments seem justified, but they carry a bitter consequence."

"What's the answer?" I ask.

"I AM the answer," He says. "I bind up the brokenhearted. I proclaim freedom for the captives and release from darkness for the prisoners. I am hope for the hopeless. And the wellspring of life for the hurting. Those who turn to Me will no longer stumble in darkness. I desire to bring them life and life more abundantly."

The weight of His words pierces my heart.

"Lord, I want to partner with you in the restoration process. I am all too familiar with my brokenness and want to see others free."

A smile appears on His face; He is pleased with my answer. "Very well," He says. "Let's work at it together."

I offer another question. "Lord, how do You feel when Your children carry an offense against You? How does it impact Your heart?"

"You ask a deep question," He replies. "Many of my children are blind to offenses they carry. They deny that they are offended and continue their relationship as if nothing is wrong. They don't realize their walk is hindered, as though they have rocks in their shoes. Left unattended, the offense turns into judgments against My character and hinders love. Doubt quickly sets in and casts a shadow on anything I do for them. They then wonder why growth is impeded.

"Let me tell you a story," He says.

"There was once a young prince who had subjects who loved and cared for Him. Everyone was happy and thriving. One day, hired thugs from a rival kingdom began to spread rumors about the Prince. At first, no one listened, so they hired more thugs to spread the lies. Pretty soon, people started believing the rumors. They stopped talking to the Prince. They turned away when He was near. The Prince did nothing but promote good laws and listen to their grievances. However, the hearts of the people grew cold and indifferent. The Prince sent heralds to proclaim His goodness. It helped; some turned back.

"A few of the people asked the Prince for help understanding. They spent time working out their doubts and pain. Those who did were soon back on track and in love with the Prince. They enjoyed the relationship and quickly recognized the hand of the Prince in their lives.

"Those who ignored the offense grew cold and indifferent; their passion and zeal faded.

"Sometime later, the rival kingdom decided to launch an attack. Disgruntled town folk eagerly signed up to partner with the enemy. The very people the Prince loved turned on Him and attacked the town, its people, and its army. How did it come to this?

"Satan's strategies haven't changed much; he used the same tactics in Heaven." (See Revelation 12:7-9). "When I see a heart polluted in this way, I work to gently restore it through repentance and love."

"That was a sad story," I say. "I can only imagine how it hurts Your heart." Convicted, I add, "Lord, I am so sorry I was once one of those people. Your leadership is amazing."

Jesus looks at me and says, "You have worked through your offenses and judgments. You are on track with My purposes. You are not late or behind schedule."

I thank Him for a great morning and end my breakfast time.

This restaurant is one of my favorite places to meet and talk with Jesus. I have returned here scores of times and have wonderful times with my Lord here. I invite you to do the same.

IT'S YOUR TURN TO PRACTICE

Engage Jesus by first priming the pump with your imagination. Envision yourself at the restaurant described in the story above. What does it look like to you? Walk around and take in as much of the scene as possible. Then invite the Holy Spirit to take over. Give it to Him and watch for a new living flow. Give yourself the freedom to enjoy it.

The following are sample questions to ask Jesus during your conversation.

1. "Pass the rolls, please."

2. What are some ways I can learn to live out of Your voice each day?

3. Are there any areas of offense in my heart that You want me to address?

4. Are there any areas of brokenness in my heart that You want to heal?

5. What are ways we can enjoy even deeper fellowship?

6. What else do You want to show me from this encounter?

Chapter 8

RESTAURANT ON A HILL – THE PROMOTION

I have become accustomed to the Restaurant after many subsequent visits. Therefore, I am surprised to see a second floor on the once "roofless" building. *How strange; that was not there before ... or was it?* I ponder this mystery as I approach the maître d' station cautiously. He is a cheerful, tall man who says, "Good morning. This way please."

I follow him up a staircase to the once-invisible second floor. I walk past the dining tables to the balcony, eager to meet Jesus for breakfast. The King is waiting, sitting at a table full of all kinds of delicious-looking foods. There are pastries, freshly baked loaves of bread, jams, various fruits, omelets, and pitchers of steaming hot liquid (I hope coffee).

This is a feast!

Even though food always captures my attention, I can't help but wonder about this second floor. The patio I usually frequent is below us.

"Good morning," I start with a big smile. "Could we do this again after I die? Even if it doesn't exist there and needs to be built, can we do it? This is so amazing!"

"Perhaps it does exist already," He says, challenging me. "I give glimpses into Heaven for those who look for it."

I reply, "So, the 'elephant in the room' question is ..."

"Go ahead," He responds.

"Why are we on a floor which was invisible before?"

"Why do you think?" He asks.

Pondering the question, I respond, "Well ... it's elevated, and it's a higher place. My guess is some type of increase or promotion."

"You got it," He affirms. "I am giving you an increase in the spirit realm. A promotion of sorts. If you put the clues together, it's an elevated place of intimacy. You can't take others where you haven't been. So, I am increasing your ability to take people into greater realms of intimacy with Me. Breakfast with a King."

"I like the title," I respond with a grin. "Thank you, my King, Big Brother, Victorious One, One Who conquered death for —" I stop mid-sentence as He hands me something.

"What is this?" I ask, extending my hand to receive the gift. It's a gold ring interlaced with a regal purple pattern.

"Try it on." He says. "It goes on the right hand."

It is royal-looking with unparalleled artistry. It fits perfectly as I slide it on my finger.

I reply, "It is the most beautiful ring I have ever seen. What kind of ring is it?"

He begins to fill in the details. "It's a signet ring. In times past, it was how power and authority were transferred to one's rightful heir or to a delegate. The delegate could then do business on his behalf. A delegate used the King's ring to seal and legalize a transaction and authenticate important correspondence. I am giving you an extension of My authority as you minister and conduct Heaven's business on Earth. You will be doing so on My behalf."

What you bind on earth will be bound in Heaven. What is loosed on earth will be loosed in Heaven.

"I don't know what to say," I mumble. "It's beyond words."

Beyond the beauty of it, and the craftsmanship, the ring conveys the trust of the King.

"I am honored You trust me to carry out Kingdom business," I say. "I intend to use it with grace and wisdom."

IT'S YOUR TURN TO PRACTICE

What would an increase look like for you in your revelatory gift? What would it be like for your ability to see into the spirit realm, to interpret dreams, or see angels? How would it enhance your walk with the Lord? Use your imagination to see yourself operating at an elevated level. Fan this flame inside yourself. Ask Him for it and be encouraged; God wants to give it to you (see Matthew 7:11).

Begin to journal with God and step into a setting like the restaurant. By faith, sit down with Jesus and begin to discuss areas in which you would like to see an increase in your life. The following are examples of questions to ask Him.

1. In what areas would You like to see me advance and excel?

2. How can I increase my desire and zeal for spiritual things?

3. What are some practical things I can do to see an increase in that area?

4. What hinders me?

5. What other adventures await today?

Chapter 9

THE LIBRARY

Not far down the hill from the restaurant described in the previous section is a library. It has a row of white marble colonnades supporting a curved roof. Curved marble steps extend down from the porch in tiers to the ground level. My guess is it would be classified as ancient Greek architecture.

I sit on the steps and wait for my King. *I hope He meets me here.* A voice echoes from inside the building, "Good morning, I'm in the sitting area inside." I rush up the remaining steps.

At the top of the stairs, I feel a refreshing breeze coming from the other end of the building through an archway open to the outside. Rows of shelves line the room parallel to each other, extending its length.

I see a simple wooden washbasin. I take the opportunity to wash my hands and dry them with a towel hanging from the side.

I set off to search for the sitting room. Soon my heart has a burning sensation; a feeling of love and acceptance floods my consciousness. I must be getting closer.

There is a room to the left with a fireplace containing a warm, welcoming fire. Comfortable-looking chairs are set near mahogany end tables. Bookshelves line the walls of this room.

I see Jesus bathed in a soft light, sipping a drink with a book in His hand. Scars on his upper wrist mark His identity.

"Welcome, come in," He says. He stands to hug me and motions for me to have a seat.

I kneel before Him, head to the ground.

"Thank you for your worship," He says.

"Lord, I'm content to remain in this position when we talk," I respond.

"OK, suit yourself, but the chair is much more comfortable," He says with a grin. "I see your heart. It's OK, you can relax in My presence."

I get up and take a seat. Strange, the seat adjusts automatically and gets a bit more comfortable. *I need one of these in my office!*

"Lord, when I imagine Your throne in Heaven, I picture it with a stylish design made out of polished marble or stone. However, isn't it terribly uncomfortable? Wouldn't You rather have a reclining, comfortable, Laz-E-Boy throne instead?"

He laughs and says, "No, I like My chair, thank you anyway."

I continue playfully, "We could get You a reclining one with a majestic look to it."

"I love your sense of humor, son."

Curious, I ask, "What is the favorite drink of the King above all kings, and what are You reading?"

"It's a homemade tea prepared the way my mother made it when I was young," He says. "As for this book—" He holds it up—"this is a collection of some of my favorite chapters from your life, some of them not yet experienced by you." He locks eyes with me.

To avoid the intensity of it, I probe further, "So, these books contain life stories?"

"Yes, each book contains significant times in people's lives" (see Psalm 139:16). "This room serves as a testimony to the faithfulness of God's servants. Stories of heroism, faith, bravery, hope, sacrifice, love, miracles, desperation, and martyrdom can be found here. Most of these stories you won't find in history books. The world doesn't remember them as heroes, yet Heaven does.

"Many of those in these stories have monuments, gardens, and beautiful tributes there. They are forever etched into the fabric and culture of Heaven."

"It's too bad those living can't read these stories to get inspired," I respond, surveying the room. "It's almost too late when in Heaven. How many people have said, 'If I would have only …?' This stuff needs to be available to those alive now to build faith, hope, and courage."

"Maybe you should write about them," He says. "You are free to see any here by faith. You have access." Jesus motions toward the books. "Go ahead, take a look around."

I browse through an aisle until I find a book that looks interesting and take it to a nearby chair on the balcony. I am momentarily distracted by the beauty of the landscape and cascading mountains in every direction. After long moments in silence, I open the book, sit down, and begin to read.

Soon I find myself immersed in what I am reading, as though I am part of it. However, I am not seen by anyone in the story.

I see a tall African man on his knees crying out to God for courage. He's speaking another language, but I can understand it. He is saying, "Oh God, give me strength not to be a coward. My village needs me, my family needs me. I want to be strong, but I'm really terrified they will catch us. Oh, help me! Make me as bold as a lion and agile as a panther! Give me Your strength."

His prayers continue like this for a while until he finishes, stands up, takes a deep breath, and begins to walk back to his village. The scene changes and he is moving from hut to hut, waking up the inhabitants, shouting, "You must wake, they are almost here, get up, get up!" in an authoritative voice.

The scene changes again, and a lot of people follow him out of the village. He rescues them all.

Back in the library, I hear a familiar voice say, "He saved a lot of people that day from certain death. The village huts were burned shortly after. He felt My prompting to move, obeyed it, asked for courage and acted. He was My instrument for the rescue. Was it a historic act? It was for the people."

I close the book and return my gaze to the common area of the library. Jesus is standing on the balcony looking over the edge. He is studying it as if He is looking for something. I say goodbye and leave to go to work.

IT'S YOUR TURN TO PRACTICE

Are the events of our lives really written in a book? Let's explore this intriguing question. In the book of Psalms, we read about times when King David expressed intense sorrow to God. One such time was when he was captured by the Philistines. He was at the time a prisoner of war. He cried out to God (literally I suppose) and wrote the following Scripture:

---

*YOU HAVE TAKEN ACCOUNT OF MY WANDERINGS;
PUT MY TEARS IN YOUR BOTTLE. ARE THEY NOT
RECORDED IN YOUR BOOK? (PSALM 56:8 NASB)*

The fact that God remembers us in our suffering is very comforting. Often people accuse God of being distant. However, God knows each of His children intimately, and every tear is meaningful to Him, just as is every triumph.

We know victories are equally important as we read the Hall of Faith chapter (see Hebrews 11:4-12). God went to great lengths to call out and give credit to people's heroic acts of faith. In the same way, He knows and rejoices in our victories.

Use the library encounter described above as a doorway or a picture on the wall (as in the former reference to *The Chronicles of Narnia: Prince Caspian* movie). Go ahead and picture yourself there. Sit with Jesus and have early-morning coffee—or tea. Then invite the Holy Spirit to take over the flow. Write what He says to you.

The following are sample questions to ask Jesus.

1. Is it true You empathize with difficult times in my life? Are my tears stored in Your bottle?

2. What about victories and triumphs? Do You store those somewhere too?

3. What dreams should I be pursuing?

4. Picture yourself accomplishing the dream He gives you. Then work backward to your present situation.

a. List potential "roads" you can travel to obtain this dream. What are the opportunities?

b. Are there any obstacles that impede progress?

c. What inspiration do I need to overcome the obstacle(s)?

d. Who do I need around me to make it happen?

e. What skills or experience should the team have?

5. Are there any stories found in this library that would encourage me in my circumstances? If so, please show them to me.

Chapter 10

THE GREAT FALLS

I start my journal time with anticipation that Jesus is going to take me to a different place this morning. I eagerly wait, pretending to be patient.

I eventually see Jesus. He gives me a hug and wishes me happy birthday. When I get close to Him, my heart begins to melt like butter in a microwave.

He says, "Before you watch the video they put together for you" (my wife and daughter Bethany compiled a birthday encouragement video from friends and family), "just know I am your biggest fan! I always will be."

Then an old Kent Henry song pops into my head. Kent starts singing the following words spontaneously:

I am for you, more than you could ever know.
I haven't left you an orphan, keep moving on;
Your heart in my hand. Have you forgotten now?
I am the great I Am, the great I Am.
I can heal your greatest hurt ...
(Kent Henry, *Awesome in this Place*, 1993)

In tears I respond, "Thank you, Lord, You are good at making me cry unexpectedly."

"I want to show you something," He says.

Suddenly we are walking on a street filled with people. Everything is immaculate, colorful, vibrant. The people are not all the way there, it's like they are out of phase; it's easy to see through them. They don't see Jesus or me as we walk next to them. I see smiles on their faces, though. They seem happy. I hurry to catch up with the faster gait of Jesus.

I see a strange sign to my right. It's not a typical metal street sign. Instead, it's a holographic sign of a tall waterfall. Water is flowing off of it somehow and spilling onto the ground, only to disappear upon contact. A cool-looking font reads, "Great Falls," followed by an arrow to the left.

We continue to walk in the direction of the falls. Jesus adds, "You're going to like this."

I begin to hear the sound of a thundering waterfall. The force of it shakes the ground. A river from a higher source tips thousands of gallons of water over a precarious ledge every second.

The walkway we're standing on is midway up the ledge. The water looks bright, crisp, and refreshing as it sprays. I hear laughter, but I don't see the source. It sounds like it's coming from the Great Falls. My jaw drops as I gaze at people riding down the falls on surfboards. It appears both terrifying and exciting at the same time. Those who complete tricks get a high five from their friends. I can only imagine what "no limitations" means with an upgraded, resurrected body.

Jesus is thoroughly enjoying this. He laughs as people do amazing tricks or wipe out. He points to a location at the bottom and says, "There they watch a hologram replay and share it with their friends."

Jesus and I drift into a conversation about challenges I'm facing. I always feel better after getting His perspective. Afterward, He looks toward the waterfall and says, "It's your turn."

I take a deep breath and say, "OK, let's do it!"

I follow Him up a steep hill on the backside of the waterfall. Soon we're climbing a series of rocks that form a rough staircase. The sound of rushing waters increases as we ascend. After a lot of climbing we finally reach the summit. There is a fast-moving stream dumping thousands of gallons of water over a sheer cliff. Off to the side is a rack of colorful surfboards available for the taking.

I start to have second thoughts as I preview the distance to the bottom. Aware of my hesitation, Jesus says, "You have to trust me as you ride it down. You can do this."

I pick a colorful board, position it near a convenient overhanging tree branch, and get on. Like a snowboard, there are stirrups for my feet. I feel the power of the water pulling me away from the safe tree branch. I see Jesus next to me on His board, effortlessly defying the force of the water.

"Let's go down together," He says, "on the count of three. One, two…"

I let go and ride the water. In a rush I am over the falls picking up speed. I feel weightless and wet. I catch a glimpse of Jesus laughing, fully soaked. He is spinning upside down and doing tricks on His board. It's exhilarating and scary at the same time. Near the bottom, another force of water pushes me horizontally away from the wave of water crashing down on me. This sudden momentum causes me to tumble over my board, landing safely in a slower-moving pool of water nearby. *Wow, that was intense!*

Jesus brushes the water off His face, still laughing. "Not bad for your first try," He says with a face radiating joy. An attendant hands us both towels to dry off as we get out of the water.

I say, "Thanks for the adventure, my King. You're so much fun." I get down on a knee and bow my head to show respect, then I leave to go to work.

IT'S YOUR TURN TO PRACTICE

Use the above vision as a springboard into your own encounter. From a place of peace and rest, allow the scene to come alive. Focus on Jesus and see what you see. Let the scene flow effortlessly.

Sample questions to ask Jesus.

1. What does "no limitations" mean for me?

2. This vision speaks of risk, thrill, and fun. What would You like to say to me on these topics?

3. In what ways can I have more fun with You?

4. Are there any areas of my life where I am too wound up, too uptight and serious? How can I loosen up?

5. How can I step into Your river?

Chapter 11

THE TELESCOPE ON THE BALCONY

I soon return to the balcony (described in the preceding chapter, "The Library"). Jesus is now standing there, gazing at something in the distance, looking concerned.

"Do you hear that?" He says.

I listen but don't hear anything.

"Try again," He says patiently.

Faint cries for help can be heard, "Please save us, we are desperate!" Another person's voice becomes more distinct, rising above the others, "No one loves me or wants me. Everyone is against me. God doesn't care, He is distant like my dad was. There is something wrong with me. I hate myself."

The murmurs continue along these lines with hopeless despair.

"Wow Lord, what is that?" I ask.

"These are groans and cries from the human heart. The fields are ripe for harvest, but the laborers are few. The time for revival is coming. I desire to interrupt the cycle and bring to them all I am—My salvation, My healing, My full redemption of body, soul, and spirit. In the quagmire of filth and degradation, My love shines the brightest. In the most hopeless of situations, I release freedom and bring wholeness." (Isaiah 61)

"Listen to this parable," He continues. "There was a party at a rich person's house. He spared nothing; he went all out. The large house was packed with people enjoying the festive night under the stars. The rooms were filled with laughter, music, and joy. The people were enjoying seemingly endless delicacies. The finest of wine was served. However, the Lord of the manor, the Owner, was not to be found. Instead, He was on the balcony of His bedroom, looking over the cities below with a telescope. He was weeping for the people there. His heart ached for them. Yes, He loved and enjoyed

His guests, but His gaze was elsewhere. Oh, My gem, the desire of My heart …" He laments.

The scene changes. A swarm of locusts descends on a city to devour it. They are confident they will take their spoil, filled with lust, greed, and vengeance.

Only three words are uttered by the Owner of the house. The words convey authority and power: "Not so fast!" He then summons a warrior of fearsome stature. He bows low to the Owner to await orders.

"I want it stopped," says the Owner, pointing to the swarm as it begins to consume the city. The warrior acknowledges the wish with a nod, bows and is gone; he literally vanishes.

A loud trumpet blast echoes in the distance. A short time later, chariots descend on the attackers from out of the sky. They are completely surprised, not knowing what has hit them. The fighting begins: light and darkness clash; sounds of conflict and screams of agony fill the air.

What is this pulsating, radiating power surge? It's like electricity in the air. Intuitively I know it's intercessory prayer. I see people who were tied up and carried off suddenly released, bonds breaking. I see explosive devices destroyed. I see demons of fear begin to tremble as light crashes in.

I shout, "Annihilate them!"

Then a volcano begins to suck up the enemy. It's somewhat humorous as large swaths of enemy troops, fallen and standing, are sucked into the volcano, like an anteater sucking up ants. Then the sun starts to rise on the night. Jesus, full of glory and majesty, steps over the hill and His blinding radiance fills the valley below.

The battle is over. Peace and rejoicing fill cities and nearby towns. Waves of power knock people over indiscriminately while they laugh and praise God. The sounds of praise and worship can be heard everywhere. People pray for physical healing and soon see the lame walk and dance as pain disappears and stiffness leaves. Weeping and prayers of repentance can be heard. The flames of bonfires engulf offensive material. Yes, people are getting set free en masse. More dancing can be seen. It looks like folks are having a blast; free at last. I guess this is the outcome when Heaven invades. Angels can be seen rejoicing with victory cries.

I am now back in the library, on the balcony. Jesus is smiling at me as we sit across from each other. As my heart continues to race from the action I witnessed, He gets up, hugs my neck and says, "Thanks for spending time with Me this morning. Goodbye for now."

IT'S YOUR TURN TO PRACTICE

Can you feel the intense passion the Lord has for the lost? It's a fact, mankind suffers. Ever since the fall of Adam and Eve, humanity has reaped suffering and pain from their sin. It's common for people to blame God for the pain they feel. Yet it's really just an impersonal law which demands a consequence for action. Every action has an equal and opposite reaction. Our sin reaps death, just as surely as jumping off a building activates gravity leading to sudden impact. However, God in His abundant mercy has intervened.

FOR SINS MEAGER WAGES IS DEATH, BUT GOD'S LAVISH GIFT IS LIFE ETERNAL, FOUND IN YOUR UNION WITH OUR LORD JESUS, THE ANOINTED ONE. (ROMANS 6:23 TPT)

Using your imagination, picture the scene in this vision. It's OK if it looks different. Let it happen. Take your time, don't hurry.

The following are sample questions to ask Jesus.

1. Please share with me how You feel about the lost. Impart Your passion to me.

2. Who are You highlighting in my life who is in pain emotionally, physically, spiritually?

3. What word of encouragement can I give that person? What word of knowledge can I share with them to reveal how intimate You are in their life?

4. How would You like me to pray for them?

5. Is there anything else I can do to align myself with Your heart?

Chapter 12

WAY ABOVE THE TREE LINE

It has taken a while to hike up this winding road. Mountain peaks can be seen all around with splashes of snow left on the rocky crags. It's peaceful with only occasional snaps of wind to disturb the quiet. I notice a serene mountain lake in the distance; the light from the sun seems to dance on the water. There is a flat rock nearby, an excellent place to have a sandwich and take it all in.

While sitting there unpacking, I see a familiar-looking angel 100 yards away. He's tall with a stocky build and brown hair. He looks at me as if he knows me. My heart starts to pound in my chest. I pray, "Lord, what should I do?" After a few moments, I hear a still, small voice say, "Follow him, he wants to show you something."

I take a deep breath and venture off in pursuit. I continue to walk and notice the scenery is changing. The ground, once rocky, is becoming softer under my feet. Instead of pebbles and rough stones, there now is lush, vibrant green grass. Colors look richer here; for example, the lake in the distance is a vivid blue-green. Wildflowers up ahead are purple, violet, and yellow. I see waterfalls cascading from higher ground. Sound waves are visible somehow.

Sweet fragrances fill the air. I notice jasmine, honeysuckle, and mint. My body now pulsates with energy; I feel alive. I find myself jogging, and it's exhilarating. I run a little faster. I have to jump and sprint. *Wow, I feel great!*

I come to a peaceful pool of water that collects the overflow from a nearby waterfall. There are a lot of yellow flowers here. As I focus on them, it's like they are giggling at an inside joke. There are no words, only a vibration. I fight back the urge to laugh. Soon I can't help it; I'm laughing hard, uncontrollably. When I've had my fill, I get up and begin to explore the nearby waterfall.

The water is flowing from a granite wall. There is a space between the rocks where the water separates the light into unique bands of color.

The beauty of this place is overwhelming: a fan-shaped rainbow of all colors, a blue-green pool of water fed by a waterfall, encompassed by banks of lush grass and yellow flowers.

Then I hear my name softly spoken from the light behind the waterfall. I follow the call. I hear my full name again, with "son of" followed by my dad's name "Edward," then his dad's name "Dodson." The voice keeps going, recounting the names from ten generations. Some of the titles include a trade or profession. It's only a whisper, but it's filled with extensive knowledge. It's like I hear fragments of a much broader story. The Speaker doesn't just know the names of each; He knows everything about them and speaks about them affectionately and with heartfelt emotion.

Dare I walk closer? I slowly step forward. As I do, I pass through the bands of color. My skin absorbs color on contact. New strength is imparted. I don't try to understand it beyond a guess that each color represents a "grace" or a spiritual gift of some sort.

On the other side of the color bands, I hear a voice say, "I know you well and remember My words spoken over you." Then a song begins to play, a sweet song of familiar prophetic words spoken over me when I was younger. It is too personal to share the detail here, but it instantly brings tears to my face. The words are now woven together into a beautiful poem; I wish I had a recording. By far, it is the sweetest, most personal love song I have ever heard in my life. I am undone. I begin to weep and sob.

He sings it effortlessly and finishes with, "Oh, my prophetic one, this is My hope for you, this is My love for you, this is your song. The song My heart sang over you before you were conceived. The ache of My heart is for you to know My love. My hope is that you walk in all I have for you. Know your identity in Me. I have formed and fashioned you to be a vessel of My love.

"I have a personal song for everyone who reads this. They are looking over your shoulder, reading and connecting. My love extends to them as well. Open the access portals so they can hear it. My heart is full of love and acceptance, mercy, and tenderness. It doesn't find fault. I have paid the ultimate price to erase all remembrances of sin. Let love restore identity and dignity. Let it remove the shame. I have seen how your heart strives to be and to do, how it tries to figure it all out. But I have your life in the palm of My hand.

"It's time for all these beautiful words to bud and comes into fruition, to take on a life of their own. My love for you is eternal. It is like a rushing waterway. It will flow from the bank of your mouth to bring glimpses of the Father to a fatherless generation. I will refresh them with love songs of Heaven, songs of destiny, songs of hope and encouragement."

As I continue to walk behind the waterfall, I see my Savior sitting peacefully with a smile on His face, looking at me with love; His face radiates a warm light.

HE SHINES IN DAZZLING SPLENDOR YET IS STILL SO APPROACHABLE. WITHOUT EQUAL AS HE STANDS ABOVE ALL OTHERS, OUTSTANDING AMONG TEN THOUSAND ... HOW BEAUTIFUL HIS INSIGHTS WITHOUT DISTORTION. HIS EYES REST UPON THE FULLNESS OF THE RIVER OF REVELATION, FLOWING SO CLEAN AND PURE.

LOOKING AT HIS GENTLE FACE I SEE SUCH FULLNESS OF EMOTION—WHAT A MAN! NO ONE SPEAKS WORDS SO ANOINTED AS THIS ONE. WORDS THAT BOTH PIERCE AND HEAL, WORDS LIKE LILIES DRIPPING WITH MYRRH. SEE HOW HIS HANDS HOLD UNLIMITED POWER! BUT HE NEVER USES IT IN ANGER, FOR HE IS ALWAYS HOLY, DISPLAYING HIS GLORY. (SONG OF SONGS 5-10,13-14 TPT)

He is genuinely humble and lowly of heart, yet filled with weighty splendor. I kneel low before Him, worshiping Him.

The scene slowly evaporates like a mist, and is replaced by a glass-like floor with reflections of immense color, light, and fire. The sound of myriad angels singing a harmony sweeter than the best professional choir on Earth fills the air with deep, vibrant, resounding voices. All of them adore their King with their sound.

The vantage point of the scene retreats, like a drone with a camera going higher and higher into the air with the view getting smaller as it rises. The Throne is now surrounded by galaxies, millions of them, singing to their Creator, with rhythms and a beat of their own, each echoing His splendor and glory. The familiar globe of our earth appears.

I'm then suddenly aware of my surroundings, sitting in my favorite chair in my room watching the blinking cursor on my computer screen.

IT'S YOUR TURN TO PRACTICE

Engage Jesus again and present your imagination to him. Let it flow inside of you and take over. Be still and enjoy this holy place with the Lord. Bask in His love for you. Recount the sights, colors, and sounds. Linger here undistracted. There is much more to see. Ask the Holy Spirit to take over and make it come alive. Tune into a prophetic flow and write down what He shows you.

Reflecting on the fact that He knows everything about you, and your family line, for generations back, ask:

1. What is the song You sing over me and my generational line? Show me a glimpse of Your passion. Open my ears to hear the melody.

2. What blessings, gifts, and anointings did my ancestors have that flowed down to me?

3. What more do You want to show me through this vision?

Chapter 13

CASTLE OF THE ANGELS

*O*ne night, I dreamed I saw a prodigious fortress made of solid rock on the side *of a cliff. Suddenly, I was climbing down a ladder into an entrance in the front.*

The scene changed, and I was inside the fortress. There was a great room with high ceilings. It had living areas in the far back and looked very impressive. It was comfortable despite being made mostly of rock. I did not see any people, but I continued to explore.

After seeking the Lord for its meaning, I felt it was an invitation to explore another heavenly building. So I started to journal focusing on Jesus and wrote what I saw.

"Are you coming?" Jesus calls down to me from a steep hiking trail. He's wearing a backpack. I start my assent. It takes me a while to meet up with Him. I am soon enveloped in a morning fog which adds a fresh dampness to the air.

He greets me with an exhortation. "You are not yet walking in your full authority. Are you content to relegate yourself to a conservative stance? You can step into more if you wish. Come on up, I want to show you something."

I begin hiking with Him. Then I find myself blurting out, "Can we fly instead?"

He replies, "There is faith in your words; alright then."

The ground leaves my feet as soon as the words leave His mouth. We are ascending in the air and moving fast along the trail like a drone at full speed. Visibility is obstructed by the fog. Occasionally, it lifts long enough to reveal a strange-looking monolithic wall hewn from the side of a mountain.

As we fly closer, the size of it becomes overwhelming. Details become apparent the more I gaze at it. It's a full castle sculpted out of the rock. The entrance gate is about two hundred feet in the air, and we are flying right toward it.

We land in an ancient-looking structure with a high ceiling. The erosions of time appear to be powerless against such a foreboding fortress. The walls radiate and pulsate with power.

As I'm admiring this formidable structure, Jesus is focused on something else. He says, "There is nothing like the sound of My warriors singing."

I hear nothing. I am too captivated by the two ten-foot-tall angels on either side of the entrance. When they see the Master, they both kneel in reverence. Then a welcome shout shakes the ground. It is not in English, nor is it in any language I have ever heard. I follow the reverent example of the giants and kneel as well.

I see Jesus walk over and speak to them affectionately, in an ancient dialect. Their faces glow brightly as the light of His love settles on them. They push massive stone doors open. The doors themselves could be studied for months. They are works of art etched in the granite, stories of battles and victories won. Each is approximately forty feet tall and looks to be four feet thick.

These giants then blow a horn like a ram's horn. The sound echoes throughout the hallowed halls.

I ask Jesus, "What is this place?"

"This is the Castle of the Angels," He says.

I hear rustling from within; lots of movement vibrates the floor. Jesus's countenance and clothes change suddenly before my eyes. He is no longer wearing a backpack and a brown shirt. He is now wearing kingly attire. His face fills with light and becomes radiant and fearsome, eyes blazing with fire, yet still somehow filled with love and compassion.

Ahead of Him, angel soldiers line up in military formation. The Captain of Heaven's Armies has made a surprise visit. What an honor to be here!

We now stand in a large hall with very high ceilings. The room looks like a military high command outpost. Areas of the room are organized according to a map of the earth. For example, there are stations dedicated just to Africa, containing African angels.

The angels here are fearsome warriors. No human, no matter how large, would dare challenge one. There is a device in each area projecting a 3D hologram of critical events happening on Earth.

I continue to look at the image coming from one of the projectors. I begin to see people filled with sorrow. They are being tormented, and they are in great fear.

I see angels jump into the hologram and land instantly at their destination. It appears to be some sort of dimensional jump point.

A squadron of angels lands and is met by an angry swarm of black, flying, insectile creatures. More angels make the dimensional leap. The fighting is intense; humans are being attacked by humans with these creatures on their backs.

I feel a pull toward the fight. I wonder how I could get over to the jump zone.

Jesus interrupts my thoughts with, "This is not your fight. I have not released you to it."

He motions for an angel to come and escort me somewhere.

I follow him down a hall and into a room filled with battle gear. This must be the armory. Swords and an assortment of weapons decorate the wall. He carefully selects a shield and calls me up to stand next to it. It is a simple, round wooden shield. Noticing my lack of excitement, he says, "Things are not always what they appear." Then suddenly, with a lightning-quick snap, he hurls the shield into the air.

In mid-air, it grows. The growth doesn't stop; it mushrooms to ten, twenty, thirty feet around and keeps expanding. I see entire houses fit under its covering. It's not done increasing; entire towns come under it.

"It conforms to the size of the prayer target," he says, "and protects what it surrounds.

"Through focus and continued prayer, you position it over anything you want to protect—people, towns, regions, etc. In doing so, the enemy will not see them, nor can they be attacked."

He walks over to the large shield. As it touches his hand, it returns to its original size. "This is the shield promised to you in a prophecy. Take it by faith, it's yours."

I receive it with gratitude. "Could I also have an upgraded battle ax?" I ask.

He sizes me up and says, "Try this one." It's the perfect size for my hand. The handle is leather; the double-sided axhead is filled with a soft light.

With tremendous gratitude, I thank him for the gifts.

"You were also promised a spear in a past prophecy," he says as he takes a spear down from the wall and balances it in his hand. "This weapon inflicts great damage to creatures of the darkness." With a whip of his wrist, he releases it to fly through the air. When it lands, it wraps around the target, like a metal cage.

"Wow, I have never seen anything like that before!" I say as I run down the floor to get a closer look.

"The King wants to talk to you again," the angel says. He then escorts me back to Jesus, who is talking to a high-ranking angel about developments in a region. They are pointing to an image in the hologram.

He looks at me and says, "I see my Armor Master has given you a few things. Good!"

"Oh yes, I am so excited," I reply as I proudly show off my new gifts, like a kid on Christmas morning.

"Very nice," He says as he looks over my new items. He then thanks the Armor Master, who bows low with respect and leaves.

I say to Jesus, "I have to go to work now. Thanks for the great adventure. Goodbye. "

IT'S YOUR TURN TO PRACTICE

Do angels really interact in the lives of men and women? The truth is, God has used angels in the lives of His children for millennia. The Bible contains almost three hundred verses that refer to angels. Thankfully, God has charged His angels with the task of helping us.

WHAT ROLE THEN, DO THE ANGELS HAVE? THE ANGELS ARE SPIRIT-MESSENGERS SENT BY GOD TO SERVE THOSE WHO ARE GOING TO BE SAVED. (HEBREWS 1:14 TPT)

I am alive today as the result of an angel's protection. One summer day in downtown Albuquerque, my wife met a homeless man. He seemed open to the Gospel, so she arranged for us to bring him food and witness to him. But the conversation didn't go as well as I would have liked. He became angry and started swearing. Suddenly, he pulled a large hunting knife and placed its point right onto my neck. Strangely, my wife and I were both peaceful as we looked at the jagged dagger resting on my throat.

The demons in this man began to tell me how they would love to cut up my face. We marveled as we remained in perfect peace while this was happening. Then all of a sudden, the man gasped as he looked behind us. What he saw terrified him. He quickly removed the dagger from my throat, jumped ten giant steps backward, and sheathed the large blade. His face was ashen, and he was very disturbed. He had seen something that terrified him. While he was muttering under his breath and walking around, we got up and walked toward the stoplight.

As we waited to cross the street, he came again, and full-force punched me in the chest. After we crossed the street, he came running—this time with his sandals in his hand, crying, "I'm sorry! I really want to know Jesus!"

I retold him the Gospel message. This angered him again as he walked back toward the library where we had first met, loosing profanities along the way. We took this as our cue to vacate as the peace we had started to lift. We left in a hurry, taking a different route back to my office.

When my wife got home, there was a message on our answering machine from Maria, an intercessor sent to us from Guatemala. She had been praying earnestly for our lives. She knew by the Spirit we were in immediate danger and pleaded for God to intervene. Thankfully He did, by sending His ministering spirits to save us.

Take a moment to thank God for the angels He has assigned to you. Ask Him to give you new insights about their role in your life.

Re-engage in the castle encounter above. Allow Jesus to take you on a tour. Simply walk through the halls of this castle by faith. What is He showing you? There is much more to see here than what is described.

The following are sample questions to ask Jesus.

1. After going to the Armory, ask Him what gear He would give you. How does He want you to use it?

2. Lord, please show me the angelic activity in this place. What are the angels doing?

3. What are a few ways I can wage war effectively for Your Kingdom?

4. What other parts of the castle do You want to show me?

Chapter 14

PLAYTIME WITH PAPA

During a worship time at church, I saw a vision of stairs appearing behind the stage. I activated the scene by faith and began to ascend. I felt overwhelming love coming from a cloud of color. Hebrews 4:16 says: Let us, therefore, come boldly to the throne of grace, that we may obtain mercy and find grace to help in time of need.

I challenged myself by asking, *What would I do now if I was confident and bold in this moment?* Then a reckless thought germinated in my head: *I will run at the Throne of Grace at top speed!*

So, without thinking it through, without analyzing the pros and cons to understand possible outcomes, I began to run by faith as fast as I could directly toward the light. Speed, light, and color all became a blur until ... contact!

Papa God grabbed my arms, spun His body to match my momentum, and flung me into space with accelerating velocity. I turned into a streak of light like the warp speed from a Star Trek engine. Stars and planets passed by on my right and left. Eventually, the momentum slowed, and the tug of gravity kicked in, pulling me backward, reversing course back to the One I love.

Then contact again, safe in His arms, but then He spun and flung me back. It was exhilarating! I was laughing and noticed Papa was, too. He was thoroughly enjoying it, along with everyone else in the room. The sense was like we were in one big living room having fun with a loving Father, yet instead of throwing His son a few feet above his head (like most fathers do), God threw me a few light years.

The solo space fight continued until I was playfully on His back trying to topple Him. Yes, I agree, the thought sounds ridiculous. My odds of pinning Him were slim. Nevertheless, we were having fun, and this amused Him. Just like it brought entertainment to my heart when my three-year-old son wrestled me, convinced he could win.

Then something unexpected happened. In this playful wrestling, my appearance changed. My head was now an eagle's head on a human body. I was wearing a white doctor's coat with a stethoscope hanging around my neck.

The vision stopped; I continued to worship, pondering the encounter and the significance of my strange appearance.

IT'S YOUR TURN TO PRACTICE

Put on your favorite worship music playlist and begin to worship. Using the above vision, engage with Father God in your imagination. What is He doing? What does He say as you approach Him?

The following are sample questions to ask Father God during your two-way journaling.

1. How does my worship impact Your heart?

2. How do You enjoy being worshipped the most?

3. What are things limiting me from enjoying Your presence?

4. What false concepts have I had about You?

5. How can I abandon myself more in You?

6. In what ways are You not like my natural father?

Chapter 15

GARDEN PORTAL

During another time with the Lord, He showed me a neatly kept garden with plants of all shapes and colors. There is a walkway in the middle lined with red and purple orchids. It leads to a short waterfall that soaks nearby plants with a fine mist. To the right is a sizeable moss-covered shade tree with a wooden swing hanging from a thick branch. Fog lingers over the plants, nourishing them.

A voice says, "I am the Water of Life. I Am the one who causes My garden to grow; this is a fruitful place."

People are gathering for worship. A woman begins to play an instrument; another one sings. Beautiful sounds fill the atmosphere. I see people on cell phones inviting others to join them. Soon people begin to arrive, observing from a distance, outside the garden, some skeptical.

Others begin to dig with shovels in hard soil. Sweat is on their brow; the digging is difficult. Their efforts are met with rain from Heaven as the ground softens. Seeds are planted.

I see a car filled with people who travel away from the garden to a city with tall buildings. They enter a large bank and walk out with laundry-sized bags of cash draped across their shoulders, like Santa Claus.

An assortment of plants is purchased at a nursery and brought back in a U-Haul truck, along with rakes, shovels, and picks. The garden expansion has begun, and everyone is eager to help plant. The seeds, plants, and roots grow rapidly, aided by the moisture of the garden.

Those who planted are now in a prayer circle. As the people pray, a geyser bubbles up from the ground, like Old Faithful in Yellowstone National Park. The people laugh as it sprays them and disappears. It appears again and drenches them, like an unpredictable sprinkler system. They continue like this for some time, laughing and playing in the water—getting totally soaked.

A man leaves the group, carrying a jackhammer. He positions himself in front of a large boulder and goes to work. It begins to crack. After more hammering, he manages to free someone from inside. He wipes dirt from her and clears the tears from her eyes. The person is then welcomed and embraced by the entire group, which was praying for her release. They give her refreshing spring water to drink. A reluctant smile forms on her face and then all of a sudden, her laughter bursts forth. The group finds this funny and begins to laugh and dance.

THEN HE BROKE THROUGH AND TRANSFORMED ALL MY WAILING INTO A WHIRLING DANCE OF ECSTATIC PRAISE! HE HAS TORN THE VEIL AND LIFTED FROM ME THE SAD HEAVINESS OF MOURNING. HE WRAPPED ME IN THE GLORY GARMENTS OF GLADNESS. (PSALM 30:11 TPT)

The man moves to another rock and begins the jackhammering process again to free someone else.

The attention of the group turns toward the silhouette of a Man emerging from white light. The people kneel in respect, their faces to the ground. The Man approaches those praying and lays His hand on their heads, which results in an envelope of glory.

The scene suddenly changes. Those who were on their faces are now on a floor made of a hard glass-like substance, smooth and polished. The clean, shiny surface reflects starlight from above. It appears to be hanging on nothing.

A voice is heard saying, "Come up here, come up higher!" The people are now dressed in clothes of pure light. They begin to climb a short, almost invisible set of stairs.

Music fills the room, accompanied by the sound of thousands—no, millions—of voices. The people walk for a short distance and are so awestruck they fall on their faces again.

The voice says, "It's OK, get up, there is nothing to fear." Then the Voice, filled with authority (as if no one could ever question it), says, "I give you access to My Throne Room. I am building a staircase through you for My children to enter. Enjoy, for I have purchased it for you with My blood."

I see a slow-moving light being poured from somewhere, like water from a pitcher. Brilliant, vivid colors fill the room. There is a green, floating expanse overhead. A general sense of love and acceptance permeates the air.

It is mixed with power. Nothing seems impossible here; it's like you could do anything, go anywhere. [As I am writing this, my physical body begins to shake.]

The music of this place is like the most talented musicians playing the sweetest-sounding instruments, times ten. Now there are tall angels all around; one of them has a golden sash and intense eyes.

What has this one seen over the ages? I wonder. These eyes are pensive, mysterious, and distant. I can't hold the intense gaze; I must look away.

Now there are different-colored waves, like intermittent shock waves shot forth from a brilliant light ahead. The light starts out soft white but then alternates color. Each color, in turn, fills the room; first red, then waves of green, then waves of blue, etc. The waves engulf people in color, and they "drink" it in; then it dissipates. Some are shaking as the light of color hits them. For some, as the light hits them, it extracts black spots (like venom) until they become whole again. Some, (even men) are now pregnant with dreams. Dreams are growing inside of them full of life. I sense new growth, like buds in a forest in spring or after the rain.

The scene fades, and the people are in the garden again. They have an afterglow which lingers with them, a hint of the color they were just engulfed in. Some glow one color, some glow another. Then the vision stops.

IT'S YOUR TURN TO PRACTICE

Have you ever felt as if your efforts were like shoveling in hard, dry soil? The shovel seems to bounce off the ground. In our backyard, there is a patch of dirt that meets our gardening attempts with stubborn resistance; we labor in vain. (Or maybe I just need to work out more.) Often ministry can feel like unfruitful gardening. No matter how hard we try to plant, it seems futile.

I believe this vision was God's way of encouraging me during a fruitless time. I was in the process of building a ministry, and while it was exciting, it also was hard work with little to show for it. The vision encouraged me at the time: if our team would stick with it, we would see the downpour from Heaven and a revelatory flow.

Using the vision above, ask God to take you to the garden and unlock its mysteries. Ask for the Holy Spirit to personalize it. Go with the flow; it's OK if it looks different.

Sample questions to ask Jesus:

1. What encouragement can I glean from this vision for my life and ministry?

2. What are You are planting in my garden?

    a. How can I cooperate with the process?

    b. Is there any pruning needed?

3. Please let me experience a Throne Room encounter. Show me the colors and let me drink the splendor of it.

Chapter 16

THE WAR ROOM

I walk up a familiar rocky road, curving left as it ascends a hill. The grassy knoll at the summit reveals my favorite panoramic view. I stop to take it all in; wisps of clouds cling to mountain tops like cotton candy. Snow-capped mountains decorate the landscape as far as the eye can see.

It's breakfast time, and I am eager to share it with my friend the King at our favorite restaurant.

Change of plans? I get a hunch my Friend is not at the breakfast table. Instead, He is at a war council meeting. I am invited to join.

Instead of a restaurant scene, there is a military encampment with warrior angels. I respectfully walk closer. These mighty ones emanate power; they have a serious demeanor, yet they still make me feel welcome. I take a knee to show respect to these redoubtable ones. Thankfully they signal for me to proceed.

I walk into a courtyard space with a modest-looking fountain or bronze washbasin. I instinctively know to wash in the red water; Selah. I am reminded my entrance here is neither free nor casual. I dry my hands with a nearby towel and proceed to the door of the War Room. Two sentinels standing guard allow me to pass.

The inside of the room appears to be a NASA-like Command Center. Modern-looking TVs line the wall, but the images being projected are not flat or two-dimensional, but 3-D. When someone highlights one of them, it projects a holographic view of live events from various parts of the world.

I see Jesus nearby, discussing world affairs with someone. He motions for me to have a seat as He finishes His conversation. The room has a sense of authority and power to it. It is a place of strategic importance; I feel a bit out of place.

Many conversations are going on in this room as world events are analyzed and evaluated.

One monitor is highlighted and amplified to the point of filling a large part of the room. The scene resembles the aftermath of a hurricane—total devastation of buildings everywhere. Women are weeping, on their knees in front of what is left of their homes. Ash, burnt wood, twisted metal, and stones are all that remain.

Trucks arrive, and relief workers distribute supplies. Their smiles seem to soothe the ravished souls more than the meals they prepare. Simple acts of service and love are deeply appreciated. Desperate people respond to the love of Jesus by repenting of sins and accepting the free gift of salvation. A precious sight!

Waves of joyous celebration spread through the camp as news of the conversions travel. It's like wind blowing across wheat fields in summer.

"IN THE SAME WAY, I TELL YOU, THERE IS REJOICING IN THE PRESENCE OF THE ANGELS OF GOD OVER ONE SINNER WHO REPENTS." (LUKE 15:10 NIV)

I also get to see another scene, not as pleasant to watch. An ugly creature with tentacles drenched in blood stretches from the Middle East to the shores of America. An alarm is sounded, and angels are dispatched; light and darkness clash. Beams of light support the angels the way a chair supports its occupant. My hunch is the light is the prayers of the saints helping the battle. It's hard to follow what is happening—just blurs of light everywhere.

Bloodlust drips from this creature like saliva from a dog's tongue. It draws strength from innocent lives being sacrificed. This creature is shrewd and lurks in shadows; it hides well, planning and plotting in the darkness, waiting for the right time to strike.

FBI and CIA agents are now collaborating in a room discussing facts, details, and maps. With God-given wisdom and skill, plans are made to move in. Deep inside a harmless-looking train car there are boxes of radioactive material. The train car has supplies for making a dirty bomb. Coal and lead shield plutonium.

The train slows down and stops. Military helicopters land and men in hazmat suits begin the cleanup process; the threat has been averted. Special Forces operators raid a compound and take the planners captive.

I'm now back in the Command Center. A sense of peace is everywhere; all is well, and danger has been averted. I thank the King for showing me these things. I bow my head in respect to those mighty ones in this room. Then I leave.

IT'S YOUR TURN TO PRACTICE

Enter the war room described above by faith; picture being escorted in. What does it look like? Imagine being invited to the war table. What does Jesus show you? Allow the scene to take on a life of its own.

The following are sample questions to ask Jesus.

1. What are the enemy's plans against my family and me?

    a. How can we overturn those plans?

    b. How can I pray?

    c. What specific strategies from Heaven can I deploy?

2. What victory strategies are You showing me for my church?

    a. In what ways is the enemy attacking?

    b. What is the best prayer strategy?

3. What are the enemy's war plans for our nation? How can we resist those plans?

4. How can I bring Your righteousness and will to our country through prayer?

Chapter 17

THE HALL OF MANTLES

After pushing through the noisy distractions of my mind, I finally focus on Jesus and hear Him say, "Let's go to a different place today."

I enthusiastically agree. He reaches out His hand, eager to take me somewhere new. There is nothing safer than getting teleported by the One who created light and the laws of physics. I am confident He knows how it all works. When my hand touches His, there is a sudden flash, and instantly we are standing in front of an old-looking mountain cabin nestled between a row of ponderosa pines.

"This place is called the Hall of Mantles," He says. "It's filled with potential and contains objects representing mantles, gifts, talents, and grace to impact the world. It is a room of unused potential. Many who came before decided they could not have what I planned for them. It requires a renewed mind to enter; it requires faith to believe these things are not only attainable but can bless the world."

Turning to Jesus, I ask, "What do You mean, it requires a renewed mind to enter?"

He says, "Many people never reach their full potential because they don't change the way they think," He says. "Their limiting beliefs about themselves, others, and especially what I can do in their lives restrict progress and growth. Their patterns of thinking keep them a prisoner to the old and familiar limited beliefs."

Jesus continues, ""The room you are entering represents potential never achieved. It's a collection of grace, even powerful mantles from people who have since stepped into eternity. By faith, these things can be acquired and reactivated."

I am now very intrigued by what is inside and can't wait to enter. Jesus continues, slowly, apparently not compelled by my impatience.

"Answers often come in seed form from Heaven. For example, Albert Einstein developed the theory of relativity with the help of a God-given dream.

"George Washington Carver began prayer each day by asking the Creator to reveal secrets about plants and vegetables. He discovered three hundred uses for the peanut, including various kinds of foods, oil, paint, ink, soap, shampoo, facial cream, plastics, and many other products.

"I am the Wellspring of witty inventions and new business concepts; I know what will sell and what will not. I know how to instruct you to prosper.

"Seek Me, therefore, for revelation and ideas."

With a gesture of His hand, He motions me into the modest-looking building ahead.

The heavy door opens quietly to reveal an oversized room resembling an attic. As I enter, I notice it's hard to stand or walk, like gravity has been turned up. It takes effort not to faint due to the power filling this room.

My eyes gravitate to a white prayer shawl hanging on a nearby clothes rack. It's embroidered with colorful Jewish symbols. I wrap it around my shoulders—perhaps a little too quickly. A heavy burden now rests on my soul; a quiet desperation to pray overtakes me. The sense I get is that things are waiting to happen as the result of my prayer. I reluctantly take the garment off. I could just camp out here and be fine.

Pushing myself to explore, I continue. There are Renaissance costumes nearby. I brush my hand against one and have a series of thoughts flash across my mind, like a whisper from long ago:

God is not interested in entertainment, nor does He enjoy a good laugh. I must give up this silly desire to act and perform. It's sheer folly. I admit I have a strong passion but who would pay to watch me? Others have greater talent. I must suppress this desire and trade in my plans for my dad's. Sigh ... The thoughts trail off.

That was strange.

Against the wall lies a suit of chainmail armor a knight from the Middle Ages would have worn. A gilded sword rests on top of it. It has a leather-wrapped handle with jewels embedded at the hilt—a magnificent sword indeed.

"Your friend will like this," Jesus says. "This is an inner healing and deliverance sword. This sword is designed to bring peace through oversight and protection. It comes with an invitation to defend the weak and the oppressed."

[Perhaps a little backstory will help the reader understand the special meaning of this gift. A friend came to me for ministry. In prayer before our meeting, I received a word of knowledge that his grandfather was involved in a secret occult organization which used skull-and-cross-bone symbolism in ceremonies and in ungodly oaths. Breaking ties with this organization was significant to my friend's freedom and prosperity.

My friend confirmed his grandfather was indeed involved in a society matching that description. He told me he was also promised a sword from them, which his dad saved for him. Until this time, he had been eagerly waiting for it. God was halting that generational stronghold and replacing it with this spiritual legacy. After the following revelation was shared, my friend renounced all the ungodly oaths sworn by his ancestors. He is now happy, free, and prospering greatly in a new job and ministry.]

Jesus continues, "Tell your friend I am restoring the original intent of his bloodline, which is to protect and fight for the safety of others. Unfortunately, his ancestors once turned to occultic, secret clubs to fulfill this drive. Accepting this gift and repenting on behalf of his ancestors restores what is rightfully his and brings him back to the original purposes of his bloodline—to bring protection, peace, and freedom, rather than anger, rage, and bondage."

"Awesome, I love it," I respond. "How should I deliver this message? Do You want to test him to see if he'll choose to give up the other sword first?"

"Yes," Jesus says, "receiving this sword will require him to forsake the natural sword offered by his dad. His dad's gift unknowingly perverts the intent of the bloodline and keeps him from My highest plans."

Looking at the sword, I commit to this special delivery. "I'll deliver the message and present this spiritual sword, but only if he chooses correctly."

With my curiosity piqued, I continue to look around. Nearby I see a lectern made of rough, unfinished wood, almost like driftwood. When I stand behind it, I have an urge to preach. Thoughts about God's Word harmonize like melody, now bubbling with passion and zeal. How fun!

Nearby is a gavel resting on a round wooden block; I can't resist. As I pick it up, I'm surprised by how heavy it is. Perhaps this somehow symbolizes the weightiness of justice. I continue to look while holding the gavel, and I begin to see a courtroom. A desire to correct injustice consumes me. I need to make it right.

"The roots of that desire are deeper than you know," Jesus says. "Don't you remember your grandfather was a judge in a small town? He was good, fair, and just. He served many years in that capacity and was honorable in his verdicts. That is why you need to correct injustice and undo what the enemy started."

I rest for a moment and let the weight of the epiphany settle in my soul. After a moment of peaceful contemplation, I see a picture of an old-fashioned scale, the kind with two metal plates suspended by a chain on a metal bar. It is out of balance, tipping to one side.

"What are you going to do about it?" Jesus asks.

I don't answer. Instead, I let go of the gavel; awareness of the mantle room returns. I continue exploring.

There is a cone, perhaps a megaphone of sorts. It's very simple-looking. It was used in a time before electricity to amplify one's voice. I put it to my mouth and out of my gut flows preaching with a roar. I laugh because power and authority came from somewhere I didn't know existed. Ideas, words, and thoughts string themselves together effortlessly. They pour out of my lips with anointing and strength.

I see the message land on hearts, impacting them profoundly. Crowds swell in size, and a reputation grows, influence expands to new regions. A ministry springs forth, resulting in overseas travel. I put the cone back where I found it. I'm not sure I have the strength for more exploration.

There is a section for children's toys and games. These are designed to spark imagination, excitement, wonder, and to create a desire for God. There are computer games to capture the heart of the video generation. I wonder who will write these programs?

There is an old Etch-A-Sketch tablet. Ah … this takes me back to my childhood. [Note to the reader from a later generation: This object was rectangular, usually red, with two round dials at the bottom. They drew lines across the page based on how the knobs were turned. When you finished drawing, a slight shake erased everything.]

I notice the Etch-A-Sketch says "witty inventions" across the top. When I move the knobs, a 3D drawing appears. This one is a mechanism which raises large objects with a beam of light. I see floors of skyscrapers being built more quickly because now the contractors can lift steel in a fraction of the time. I let go of the handle, and the thought disappears.

This room has so many treasures! *Dare I ask if there is anything here for —?*

"Are you ready for this?" Jesus says, standing near something with a smile, anticipating my question.

I walk closer and notice a large quill and inkwell. I can guess what this symbolizes. "It's a Writing Mantle?" I offer with anticipation.

"If you accept this," Jesus responds, "your desire to write will increase, and you will have a heavenly grace on your words, causing them to lift your audience to new heights. Are you ready?"

It looks simple enough, just a swan feather with a point. I reach out my hand to take it.

The scene immediately changes. I see myself in a cabin writing feverishly, hands blazing across a keyboard. I am emotional; the content impacts me; at times I stop to cry. Other times, I yell and praise God while new thoughts are captured and placed in context, like puzzle pieces. Days pass at this secluded cabin. I don't sleep, nor do I receive phone calls or texts. *I have to get it done!*

I let go of the quill; the image disappears.

I am aware of the Mantle Room again. Jesus says, "Well, do you want it, knowing the work involved?"

"Absolutely," I respond resolutely. He hands me the quill, wrapped in leather.

"I look forward to your seeing your finished works," He says with a smile.

I reply, "Thank you. I look forward to it as well. Also, thank You for bringing me here. Goodnight." I give Him a hug and leave.

IT'S YOUR TURN TO PRACTICE

Enter the Mantle Room by faith. Allow Jesus to show you around. What captures your attention and tugs at your heart?
Sample questions to ask Jesus:

1. In what ways do I imitate the opinions and ideals of my culture?

2. How can I cooperate more with the process of transforming the way I think?

3. Is there a special mantle or grace You would like to impart to me from this vision?

    a. How does this relate to my current ministry or vocation?

    b. Does it involve a new direction?

    c. How do I use it effectively?

    d. Is there a timing to it?

4. What will it cost in terms of dedication, obedience, or discipline?

5. How do I walk in the fullness or maturity of it?

6. How will it impact my life and the lives of those around me?

Chapter 18

PROPHETIC ARTISAN

O ne morning during prayer, an image of a well-manicured garden comes to mind. It looks like a garden on an expensive English estate. I begin to scan the landscape for Jesus. To my surprise, I see many Jesuses. *Has Jesus been cloned?*

Each version of Him is fully engaged with a different person, walking and enjoying their company. He is giving undivided attention and love to each, as though each is the only one. This is not too difficult for an omnipresent God I suppose.

All of this is as it should be, but my heart yearns for more adventure, more thrill. I want to see more and do more than just walk in a pretty garden.

"Be careful what you ask for, you just might get it," Jesus says as He walks toward me.

He directs me to a nearby river flowing with rough, choppy water. The flow of current is so wild it could be a Class 5 rapid, the most dangerous current. The water also seems to defy gravity as it shoots straight up into the air after smashing against rocks. *Hmm ... getting in there may not be a good idea.*

"What is that?" I have to yell to make my voice heard above the noise of the water. I point to a group of strange, floating barrels of light. They are hard to make out at first but become more distinct as I watch. Each barrel is propelled into the air briefly and then disappears. They resemble a log ride at an amusement park but are made of light.

"What are those?" I ask.

"Why don't you climb into one and find out?" Jesus suggests.

"Say again?" I protest.

"But didn't You just say—" Jesus starts. Before He finishes, I relent.

"OK, OK, how does one get into this?"

He points to a log floating nearby, which soon comes within reach.

I reluctantly get in and sit down.

"You may want to hold on tight," He says as He waves His hand in an upward movement.

I am propelled like a cannonball being shot. The force is so strong I can't move a muscle. I remember His words, "Be careful what you ask for."

The sensation is like a rollercoaster. I'm not sure if there is a track under me, but the back-and-forth motion feels like being flung in the air by a trapeze artist at a circus. Instead of over-analyzing it, I purpose to enjoy the ride.

Wow, what a spectacular view! Mountains and waterfalls can be seen for miles in all directions. The river is now a small line on the ground beneath.

I gently land on a wet, sloping rock. I slide for a while until I can stand. It's time to explore my surroundings. A short path opens to a shiny street made out of clear stone. Everything looks clean and new. There are no tire marks or debris on the street. Shops lining the road are made of polished white and grey marble.

Flowerpots accent the stores. It reminds me of upscale mountain towns I've visited in Colorado. There is an empty pavilion resembling the famous opera house in Sydney, Australia, perhaps on a smaller scale. It has multiple archways in the shape of shells, each facing the same direction. I resist the urge to yell to test the acoustics.

Seats line the theater facing the stage. There are no walls, so entry is available from all sides.

As I walk in and sit down, my seat immediately conforms to my body, making it incredibly comfortable. *I need one of these at home.*

My hand rests on the armrest and activates a hologram which projects a menu into the air. It touts upcoming shows at the theater, none of which I have time to watch now.

I get up and venture out into the street and begin to walk. I notice a freestanding flight of stairs that appears to go nowhere. *I must study this;* I say to myself. *It might be worth a second look.*

People are walking up and down the wide stairs in both directions. At the top is a podium with a console. As people touch it, an invisible door opens, and they walk through. After they enter, it disappears behind them. Others arrive through it and walk down the stairs. My guess is it is a transportation device. I will return later to see where it will take me.

I am attracted to a granite rock wall surrounded by large boulders. I find a walkway that narrows into a cave hidden behind a small waterfall. There is a strange moving sidewalk, like the kind you might find in an airport terminal. I get on it and start to walk. When I feel safe, I run.

I pick up the pace, and the walkway moves at my speed. It's strange but I'm not getting tired. So, I decide to go faster. *Why am I not getting tired …?* I continue to increase my speed until everything becomes a blur. I laugh as I challenge the speed threshold.

It's exhilarating. There seems to be no limit to how fast I can go. My energy is not depleted, so I stretch myself. I continue until my legs become a blur. Then the thought occurs to me: *I don't know how to slow down.* If I jumped off, I would be flung into the nearby rock like a slingshot. I force my legs to run slower. It works, speed decreases, and I am eventually able to get off. Instead of sweating and being exhausted, I feel energized and continue my exploration.

My next stop is an outdoor gathering of people who are watching a man outside a nearby shop. The man is an artist creating art for people on demand. He first studies the person, gazing intensely into their eyes before starting his new masterpiece.

His method is to scoop up a substance that looks like gooey, liquid light. He forms it with his hands in midair. It's like watching a skilled artist painting a picture on a blank canvas, or a glass blower making beautiful 3-D artwork from the hot, glowing liquid glass. I know intuitively he paints a prophetic message of hope and encouragement.

The lady receiving his finished work is noticeably moved. The prophetic message impacts her soul profoundly. She begins to sing and dance. Others join in, and the crowd erupts into dancing and shouting. Some do not even know why, nor do they care. I join in the fun and begin to swirl people around with locked arms.

The Artisan then motions for me to come to him. His gaze is intense; he is looking into my soul and gathering information. *What does he —?* Before I finish the thought, he stops listening and begins to create.

His scoops up the lava liquid and forms it into a circular picture. I gaze at the process with anticipation. I remark to someone next to me, "I have never received prophetic art before."

He completes my art and hands it to me. It pulses with power. It's difficult to describe it, but in simple terms, it's a series of portal openings in the heavens. The painting shouts a prophetic message with authority, yet without words, "You will provide access for My people to enter heavenly realms. They will have a new template to use as they come and go as they please."

I thank this insightful artisan and leave, elated by my new treasure.

Suddenly, I become aware of my office surroundings again.

[Note to the reader: This picture was one of the motivating factors causing me to write this book. I intend to fulfill the prophetic artwork by creating access for people.]

IT'S YOUR TURN TO PRACTICE

Use the above vision to give you a new grid for a heavenly scene. It's an onramp or portal; step into it by faith and look around. The more you focus on celestial images like this, the more you will see. You can enter as many times as you wish. You will find new encounters each time you do.

The following are sample questions using the scenes of this vision.

1. Lord, please highlight the things You want me to notice in this scene.

2. Interact with the surroundings. What stands out to you?

3. Ask the Artisan to give you a prophetic word through His art.

    a. What does the artwork say to you?

    b. What is the prophetic theme?

4. Lord, what are further insights You would give me about this word?

I thank my precious wife for writing the remaining chapters of this book. In the subsequent pages, she shares some of her most intimate times with the Lord so you, the reader, can benefit from her journey toward intimacy with the Father. While the style, tone, and emphasis are noticeably different, you will be captivated by her longing for more God.

Her zeal for encounters and her rich prophetic gift makes the following sections captivating and difficult to put down. Her prophetic experiences are easy to relate to because we all have had similar questions and doubts at times. My wife's humility and passionate zeal for the Lord have resulted in astonishing dreams, angelic encounters, and heavenly visitations. She refuses to settle for anything but God's best. This drive has led her to polish her prophetic gift, which regularly blesses friends, family, and people we have the privilege of counseling.

INTRODUCTION to PART 2

I, Marcia, trust that you have been captivated by what you have read so far. My husband has been an amazing encouragement to so many. His laughter is infectious, his heart for God is enormous, and he has such a passion to see souls set free and activated to be all that God has called them to be. I have learned so much from his patience and unconditional love.

Yet, I have not always been as faith-filled as Tom and have had periods of doubt and fear that I've dealt with partially through vision and journaling. The Lord has been gracious and kind. He never gets frustrated or impatient. He is always encouraging and full of faith.

As you read, you will be listening in on a dialogue between me and the Lord. I call Him by His name and refer to Him as "You" throughout the text.

I feel vulnerable writing these things for others to see, but Tom and I share them so others will experience the healing, inspiration, intimacy, and joy He has given us through this process.

As I write this, the Lord is blessing me in the natural as I am looking at a breathtaking rainbow coming out of the clouds over the mountaintops from my upstairs window. *Thank You, Lord! Your promises are true, and Your heart is always for my good! You speak all the time; we need to be prepared to hear.*

My goal for this section of the book is for you to experience more of Him through encounters and even the struggles that I've had. My prayer is that in doing so, He would impart to you a greater understanding of your identity and authority. I think you will see a progression of my relationship with the Lord as you read about my very ordinary life.

I am reminded of a movie that will illustrate my point. *Jack the Giant Slayer* is a 2013 fantasy adventure written by Darren Lemke and Chris McQarrie. The screenplay is loosely based on the story of *Jack and the Beanstalk*. Jack discovers dangerous giants who live above the clouds. When the giants have the opportunity, they attack the humans and wreak havoc on the town below, destroying everything and everyone in their path.

[Spoiler alert:] The army bravely tries to defend the city but is powerless against the formidable giants, who crash through every barrier erected. The main character, Jack, finally takes possession of an ancient crown. This crown was created to impart authority to control the giants. As the last remnant of the resistance forces is about to wiped out, Jack steps forward with the crown, and the entire army of giants stops and kneels in submission.

In a similar way, darkness has to obey the authority imparted to the sons of God. Amen! The darkness may be powerful, but authority trumps power.

NOW YOU UNDERSTAND THAT I HAVE IMPARTED TO YOU ALL MY AUTHORITY TO TRAMPLE OVER HIS KINGDOM. YOU WILL TRAMPLE UPON EVERY DEMON BEFORE YOU AND OVERCOME EVERY POWER SATAN POSSESSES. ABSOLUTELY NOTHING WILL BE ABLE TO HARM YOU AS YOU WALK IN THIS AUTHORITY.
(LUKE 10:19 TPT)

This movie paints a beautiful picture of this verse. By wearing His authority, all forces must bow to us. It doesn't mean we overpower them (power is another thing altogether); rather it means they obey those in the royal family of God. When we choose to take our place as sons and daughters of the Most High God, we have real authority! Jesus did so much for us! The Bible says we are "a royal priesthood, a holy nation; we have the ministry of reconciliation" (1 Peter 1:9). Beloved, the question for all of us is, "Do you know who you really are?!"

Our part is to restore back to Him the reward of His suffering. He paid for healing, so we have the privilege to partner with Him to get people healed. He paid for freedom, so we are supposed to help them get free. He paid for salvation, so we are to share the Gospel and pray for people to be saved. More than that, He paid the full price for the reconciliation of all things to Himself (Acts 3:21)!

This is not a mental assent or something we just say "someday" we will do. We have to go out and, well, just do it!

I am a speech and language pathologist (therapist for short). If I want my students to take something from short-term to long-term memory, I have to help them associate it with something they already know. We need to know the Word of God is true. We need to know what God wants us to do by what

85

He has said in His Word, and to remember what God did in the past. If we're going to build from short-term to long-term memory, we also need to use our many senses—what we see, what we hear, what we smell, what we taste. After all, Jesus only did what He saw His Father do (John 5:19). Let's add some movement to it as well by being "doers of the Word, and not hearers only" (James 1:22). We can talk about healing for fifteen weeks in a class, but if we don't lay hands on the sick, we won't see anyone healed. If we go to all the seminars for inner healing and deliverance, but we don't apply those principles, then people won't be set free. If we don't share the good news of what Jesus did for us, then people will not know to come into the Kingdom.

It's like playing an instrument. When you first start, it may sound squeaky, but with proper training and practice, it will begin to sound pretty good! The more you practice, the better you play. Let's say, though, you play the violin for ten years, then you put it down for five. When you pick it up again, you may not sound quite the way you remembered. It's "by reason of use" that you grow in your ability to see, hear, and operate in the supernatural (Hebrews 5:14).

We have more authority than we realize when we agree to partner with God. My daughter Bethany was a cheerleader at a high school that was difficult to get into as a former homeschooler. We had to jump through several hoops before she could attend school there and be on the cheer team.

One day, I was washing her uniform as I usually did. When I pulled it out of the washing machine, there were ink stains all over it! I never found a pen, but my daughter tried hard not to cry as she related her concern that the uniforms only come in lots, and if she had to replace this one, the new one would likely not match. If that was the case, she might not be able to cheer with the team.

So, I looked online to find out how to take stains out. Some of the ideas began to work, and a little bit of ink was starting to come out, but overall, the situation was not looking good. The white uniform was still covered in ink.

I remembered we have authority over our realms of influence. Laundry is an area of influence I have! I took the uniform in my hands and said, "You stinkin' devil, you cannot have this! Stains, come out, in Jesus's name!" In a matter of seconds, all the stains were gone, and my daughter's uniform was completely white again—even brighter! We both were astonished and said aloud, "Did that really happen?!"

I am sure you have similar stories of God's intervention—if you were paying attention to them. He graciously takes care of us even before we aware of His existence.

I have several stories having to do with cars. Sometimes you have to lay hands on them to get them to run, particularly if you have older vehicles. Tom and I once had a Jeep Wrangler. We loved that Jeep; it was blue with a little sun symbol on the side. We would take the top off, turn up the music, and rock out to DC Talk or Toby Mac. It was so much fun!

On a particular day, we were in the mountains of Colorado near Telluride, going into the wilderness. We were following a little Suzuki. We were making fun of Suzukis because we thought Jeeps were far superior. (Jeep owners can be a bit prideful.).

The Suzuki crossed through a river without difficulty. Since we were right behind it, we did the same thing, not realizing the water was deep. When we drove in, the Jeep stalled. There was water coming up to the passenger door where I was. My thoughts turned to a bus driver I knew who got stuck in a dry riverbed during a flash flood, which swept the bus away. He and all the kids had to be rescued! I wasn't going to have any of that, so I laid my hands on the Jeep and said, "In the name of Jesus, you will start right now, and you will come out of the river!" The Jeep leapt up and out of the water right away. I don't remember how we got off the mountain, but we didn't cross that river again!

Do you know the "earth is groaning for the sons of God to be revealed" (Romans 8:18)?

Let's take the weather. I wonder about weather sometimes. Fires, floods, tsunamis, tornados ... Could it be the enemy is wreaking havoc on the earth because we haven't put our crowns on? Something to think about.

I believe Jesus will return. However, just like He did the first time, likely not at all in the way we have been expecting. I believe we actually have a part to play in that plan. He wants us to agree with Him that His Kingdom will come on the earth as it is in Heaven (Matthew 6). He wants us to occupy until He comes (Luke 19) and more than that, I believe He wants us to be His actual Body on the earth. There is more to this than we have ever understood or imagined, let me tell you!

I have a fun story about my son, Jeremiah, when he was four years old. My dad was in the hospital in Albuquerque, New Mexico. I was frantically trying to get there because I wasn't sure he would make it. The kids were little, ages three and four, so I put them in our little white 1999 Metro with terribly skinny tires, and we proceeded to drive the seven hundred miles from Dallas to go see my dad.

That was a lot for our tiny car under normal circumstances, but this time we were traveling through an ice storm! The wind was whipping us around, and the ice was super thick on the road. Sleet was coming down, and the trucks that passed us were throwing ice onto my windshield. I kept thinking perhaps I should turn around, but if I did, I'd only face the same danger. If I kept going, it might just get better.

I drove past Amarillo, and it didn't get better. In fact, it got worse, but by then, we were in the middle of literally nowhere! It was bad. I was praying in the Spirit, praying and praying in the Spirit, while my emotions were not in the Spirit at all! I said aloud, "Lord, just keep us safe and help us get there!" That's when I heard a tiny voice from the back seat say, "Jesus, You're the BIGGEST!"

I almost cry every time I think about that moment. The wind stopped almost immediately. It was like the ice on the road just melted, and we drove the rest of the way in peace.

The Bible says, "As He is, so are we in this world" (1 John 4:17). Jesus calmed the storm (Mark 4:35-41). Jeremiah, even at age four, did too!

The "same Spirit Who raised Jesus Christ from the dead lives in us" (Romans 8:11). He said, "In Christ, we are partakers of the divine nature" (2 Peter 1:4).

At the tower of Babel (Genesis 11), He said, "Nothing will be impossible for them" so He confounded their language. These were pagan, unredeemed people who had no regard for God. How much more is this true of those of us, who have His Spirit, His divine nature, and the same Spirit who raised Jesus Christ from the dead!

He is the Vine; we are the branches (John 15:5). We are extensions of Him. He's the Head, we are the body. He said, "Father, I desire that they may be one as You and I are One" (John 17:21).

Can you really wrap your mind around that?

It's time to make sure of the promises He has for us. Because of His promises, we are no longer servants, but joint heirs with Him (Romans 8:17). That means we have everything He has (Ephesians 2:6)! He's "raised us together in the heavenly places in Christ Jesus." Where's Jesus? He's seated "at the right hand of the Father, far above all power and dominion, rulers and authorities" (Hebrews 12).

He is "Christ in us, the hope of glory!" (Colossians 1:12)

The anointed One lives in us; that makes us anointed, too. We are kings and priests (Revelation 1:6). Kings have authority over their realms of influence. Let me tell you, it's more than laundry! He said, "greater works will we do" (John 14:12). This is in the Bible, folks!

I'm ready to make the change. How about you? I want to put off everything that hinders. I want to change the way I think about myself. I want to stop focusing on my shortcomings. I want to focus on the Truth of what

He came to do. He deserves the reward for His suffering. For the "joy set before Him, He endured the cross" (Hebrews 12:12), knowing He was gaining us as His inheritance!

That's what this book is really about: giving Jesus the reward of His suffering with our hearts completely ravished by His love. The supernatural life begins and ends in the secret place.

PLUNGE IN

I see myself standing on a pier, the wind blowing in my face. The sun is setting. I am breathing in the beauty of all the colors of the sky and the fragrance of salty air perfumed with sweet-smelling flowers I cannot identify. You are walking toward me on the water. You smile and invite me to plunge in.

I have fears of creatures unknown; of cold water; of drowning; of not being adequately dressed. What if I can't see anything?

Yet … the deep is exciting. It has mysteries that cannot be seen unless I take the risk. Becoming love, becoming like You, costs everything.

"The waves are getting higher, Lord," I complain as the winds pick up. I take off my glasses. I shed my jacket and shoes and leave them on the pier. "I am coming in, Lord, and not holding anything back. HELP me, Lord!"

The plunge … water engulfing and wrapping around me now. It's an awkward feeling as my arms and feet are flailing, lighter, now gasping for air. *Where is He?* I wonder.

Then I locate the One my heart desires. You catch me and bring me to the surface. You show me the water is calm.

I lean against Your chest—my hair is wet and splattered across Your face. "I did it! I did it!" We begin to laugh together. "I heard You beckon, and I responded! Even though it seemed risky."

I can see clearly; the sun is dancing on the water.

"Are you ready?" You say. Smiling, I nod as You pull me under, not just barely beneath the surface, but way, way under.

I can breathe; I can see! It's so very peaceful here. Even though we are well below the surface, I can see rainbow colors dancing in wave patterns in the water. I look at all kinds of marine life: humpback whales swim by, fish are innumerable, and an octopus propels itself along.

There's the treasure chest. The one You showed me years ago, the one I was not ready to open. This time, we are approaching it from another angle. It is buried halfway in the sand and decorated with translucent hues of greens and blues.

A divinely orchestrated song begins to play in my room in the natural as I draw close to the treasure chest in the spirit. I am speechless as I recognize His voice filling my room. The Lover of my soul begins to sing over me through the prophetic worship song of Kimberly Rivera:

I've been waiting for you more than you could ever ask, more than you could ever imagine;
There's so much more I have for you;
You've only just seen the tip of the iceberg, but it goes so broad, so deep, so high;
You've only just had a taste of Me;
But wait until I bring out all that I have for you;
I'm going to overwhelm you. I AM an overwhelming flood;
So be overwhelmed by My loving-kindness.
(Kimberly and Alberto Rivera, *Wide Open*, 2014)

I wipe tears from my face as I say, "I *am* overwhelmed. Your timing is amazing, Lord. That was beautiful."

I continue to look at the treasure chest which is now within arm's reach. I tell You, "You are so much more than I can ever imagine. I am Yours. I want to be Your bride. I want to be Your true love—and for You to be mine."

There's a lock on the chest. I hear You say, "You have been given the keys of the Kingdom."

"Lord, why am I afraid?" I say as I examine my heart. "I am afraid the chest will be empty or have so little because I have been so faithless."

"I have given you the keys of the Kingdom, My beautiful Love Dove," You say tenderly. "Yes, you are Mine. I love you! Everything I have is yours, My darling dove.

"Every single thing is yours, My beautiful one. Let Me tell you a truth. Eyes on Me now, Love. Eyes on Me. Whatever you see, you can not only have, but you can be. Look at Me with dove's eyes."

"I am undone, Lord," I reply. "Such knowledge is too wonderful for me! I want to be where You are Lord, every day, forever …"

I see myself swimming around and around, joyfully, with a mermaid tail! It is shimmery and fun! I am adapting to the atmosphere in the depths. I embrace You tightly, and we swim around and around and around. I want to open the chest, but I don't want to leave this place.

"THANK YOU to the One who was, and is, and is to come," I declare. "All glory and honor and power are Yours, Lord. You are the great I AM!"

Jesus, Yeshua, Yahweh. Yod Hey Vav Hey. Behold the Hand, Behold the Nail! Selah.

YOU WILL MAKE KNOWN TO ME THE PATH OF LIFE.
IN YOUR PRESENCE IS FULLNESS OF JOY; IN YOUR
RIGHT HAND ARE PLEASURES EVERMORE!
(PSALM 16:11 ESV)

I don't want to open the chest because You are the Treasure, Lord!

IT'S YOUR TURN TO PRACTICE

Enter this scene by faith. Picture yourself on a pier. You may want to have soft, instrumental music in the background. Allow yourself to experience the atmosphere with all of your spiritual senses. What do you feel? What do you smell? What do you see? What do you hear? Can you taste anything? Write these down. Then wait.

Look and keep on looking. Hear and keep on listening. Meditate on any emotions that start to well up. Write down any thoughts that come to you, even if they seem ridiculous. You can test these later with the Scriptures. For now, you are practicing the Presence. Receive it with gladness.

The Bereans in Acts 17:11 "received the message with great eagerness and examined the Scriptures every day to see if what Paul said was true."

Here are some sample questions for the Lord using the scenes of this vision:

1. Lord, is there anything that is holding me back in my relationship with You?

2. In what ways have my fears hindered our relationship? How would You like me to deal with those fears?

3. Ask God what this means: "Whatever you see, you can not only have, but you can be."

   a. What do You want me to see, have, or be today?

   b. How can I apply this encounter to my life?

   c. What are some practical next steps?

   d. Ask God for a surprise gift in your unique love language.

   e. What is His personal, loving, intimate name for you?

Chapter 20

THE FLYING CARPET

*W*hy am I thinking about flying carpets? I see funny shoes as well.
I hear You say, "Things on Earth are a type and shadow of things in Heaven, My love. Even unbelievers can see glimpses of heavenly realms."

You are stretching me with this revelation.

"OK. So, Lord," I say emphatically, "I want to go on a flying-carpet ride with You!"

Tapestry. You are wearing what looks like a tapestry. Intricate, meticulously crafted.

I see women in black headscarves putting something in a hearse. "What is this?" I wonder out loud.

You are taking me above that scene on a carpet that matches Your attire, changing my focus. You are smiling, cross-legged, eating grapes and pomegranates. There is purple juice on Your hands. I take a pomegranate too, and now there's purple juice all over my hands and face! You squish some juice on me, and we laugh and laugh.

Whoa. The ride is getting bumpy, but it's a gorgeous day! No fears of falling or crashing—just focused on being with You! I feel like a little girl! I am wearing a light and airy pink chiffon outfit. You ask, "Do you want to see My garden?"

"Oh yes, Lord," I respond. We peer over the side of the carpet while lying on our stomachs.

There are miles and miles of beautiful carpets of blossoms and gradients of green farther than the eye can see. They change color as we fly over them.

"I cherish the times You've brought me to Your garden and shown me some of Your plants, Lord. May we go down now and look around?" I ask longingly.

I notice that You have a white turban on Your head, and I now have a small blue and white one.

Selah. "Look it up, love," You say.

AND YOU SHALL SET THE TURBAN ON HIS HEAD AND PUT THE HOLY CROWN ON THE TURBAN. (EXODUS 29:6 NASB)

THEN I SAID, "PUT A CLEAN TURBAN ON HIS HEAD." SO, THEY PUT A CLEAN TURBAN ON HIS HEAD AND CLOTHED HIM WHILE THE ANGEL OF THE LORD STOOD BY. THE ANGEL OF THE LORD GAVE CHARGE TO JOSHUA: THIS IS WHAT THE LORD ALMIGHTY SAYS, "IF YOU WALK IN OBEDIENCE TO ME AND KEEP MY REQUIREMENTS, THEN YOU WILL GOVERN MY HOUSE AND HAVE CHARGE OF MY COURTS, AND I WILL GIVE YOU A PLACE AMONG THESE STANDING HERE." (ZECHARIAH 3:5 NIV)

Turban—one of the priestly garments (Exodus 28:4); to stop, to rule, to bind up, to gird about, to govern, healer.

THEY TIED IT TO A LACE OF BLUE TO FASTEN IT TO THE TURBAN ABOVE. (EXODUS 39:31 KJV)

"Interesting, Lord. Priestly. Mine even has the blue lace! Wow. What does it look like, Lord, to be priestly or a to be a king?"

"Set apart. A turban covers your mind. When you're a king, your mind is on the Kingdom."

I hear You say, "It costs a great price to become a merchant ship and not just a mediocre vessel." I am surprised by this Scripture found in Proverbs 31:14-15. Selah (this means to think about it carefully).

IT'S YOUR TURN TO PRACTICE

Position yourself to go on an adventure with the Lord. By engaging the scene above, ask the Lord to take you on a flying-carpet ride! Lie on your belly and look over the side.

These are sample questions to ask.

1. Is there a place that He highlights? What do you see? Ask the Lord if He will take you there.

2. Picture yourself with a turban on your head. Ask the Lord what He is saying about your authority. What does it mean to be a priest and a king?

3. Remember to notice sights, sounds, fragrances. Watch for highlights. Inquire of the Lord about things that stand out.

4. Meditate on Proverbs 31:14. What does this mean to you? Are you willing to pay the price that is required of kings and priests in order to become a distribution channel of Kingdom resources?

Chapter 21

FOLLOWING THE LEADER

I am standing on the beach. The sky is overcast, but there are visible shades of blue. It is early morning, the waves are trickling in, and their sound is fainter than expected in the background. I see You, my precious Lord, in the distance, beckoning.

"Come with Me."

MY BELOVED SPOKE AND SAID TO ME, "ARISE MY DARLING, MY BEAUTIFUL ONE, COME WITH ME. SEE! THE WINTER IS PAST; THE RAINS ARE OVER AND GONE. FLOWERS APPEAR ON THE EARTH; THE SEASON OF SINGING HAS COME; THE COOING OF DOVES IS HEARD IN OUR LAND. THE FIG TREE FORMS ITS EARLY FRUIT; THE BLOSSOMING VINES SPREAD THEIR FRAGRANCE. ARISE, COME MY DARLING; MY BEAUTIFUL ONE, COME WITH ME." (SONG OF SONGS 2:10-13 NIV)

You have a smile on Your face as You walk purposefully; I hurry to catch up to You. I look down to see if I am appropriately dressed. OK, good. I am wearing a white cotton dress and bare feet. I hear the splash and squish of mud as I run to catch up to You.

You are heading into a jungle. It looks dark and dense in there. I would not ever venture in there if You were not with me.

There is a totem pole with a formidable-looking face. It topples as You walk past it. There's an ominous black python with grey-and-yellow diamond shapes slithering slowly along the ground. You step on it, and You tell me to do whatever You do.

As I step on it, I hear it groan, and it propels me up to another level on the path.

"Wow, Lord," I respond with a new epiphany, "since my eyes were on You, I wasn't afraid."

We continue climbing in this muddy terrain with dense foliage. Both hands and feet are needed as parts of the climb require stretching. We do not have any climbing gear, and my feet are still bare.

When we stop in a meadow, You are not dirty at all, but I have smudges on my face, though my dress is still pure white. You touch my cheek—liquid Love fills my whole being. I lean into Your hand. The smudges are gone. I want to linger, but You can't wait to bring me to a new place.

"But Lord, You are my Treasure. I want to be with You ... in any place," I tell the One my soul loves. You pull me close and kiss the top of my head as You embrace me tightly.

I see myself now dressed in a strikingly white wedding gown, following You under a garden gate that looks like a keyhole. I have to stoop low to get under the gate, but when I push through, You are standing next to a crystal-clear river.

I stop to soak it all in and say, "Can we stop here for a while?" I am elated to see blue and gray mountains decorating the horizon. You gesture for me to follow. I look down at my dress, thankful that it is still white and not dirty, then my eyes turn toward my footwear. "More like Cinderella slippers than hiking boots," I joke.

A Scripture then comes to mind: "Humble yourselves before the Lord, and He will lift you up" (James 4:10). I sense You saying that I shouldn't wait for everything to be perfect before stepping out in faith.

IT'S YOUR TURN TO PRACTICE

Have you ever found yourself taking charge when you really should be following? Instead of waiting for Him, we find ourselves way ahead, wondering if He will bless our actions. There is a peace that comes, however, when we know we are following His lead. We can know the destination is going to be good and often He reveals more to us about our identity.

Spend time quieting yourself before the Lord and remove distractions. Ask the Lord to take you under the gate (described above) through the keyhole. Ask Him what opens the door.

Be aware of your environment. Write down as many details as you can. They may be metaphors.

1. Ask Him what you are wearing during this encounter. Are you clothed in robes of righteousness? (Galatians 3:27) See Appendix C if you have questions.

2. Is there a scary place that He is helping you to overcome? As in this vision, I kept my eyes on the Lord and followed Him to step on a python that propelled me to a new place. What do you need to overcome?

Chapter 22

NARROW PASSAGEWAY

I see myself going into the garden where the Lord and I have met many times before. It is hard to get in without stooping down because the trellis at the entrance is overrun with roses. It looks like it hasn't been tended in a while.

"No Lord, I really have not been tending Your garden. My job has consumed me," I say apologetically.

Roses are beautiful and smell incredible, yet they have thorns. Roses do best when pruned. Then they can multiply.

I approach the narrow entrance. I cautiously squeeze my body past the sharp thorns. On the other side, I seem much more prominent. "Hmm. A small, humble overgrown opening causes me to be a giant?" Selah.

ENTER THROUGH THE NARROW GATE ... HOWEVER,
SMALL IS THE GATE AND NARROW THE ROAD THAT
LEADS TO LIFE, AND ONLY A FEW FIND IT.
(MATTHEW 7:13-14 NASB)

My body is too big (like Alice in Wonderland) for all the plants in this place. I seem to be pushing them off tables and shelves with every movement. Did I go to the same familiar garden or another location? The confusion comes from not hiding the Word in my heart, and it comes from double-mindedness.

"Lord, I certainly have been double-minded about many things," I confess.

"Lord, I am struggling with this. I feel so much like my job has consumed my mind. I feel a bit like the day of reckoning has come for all that I didn't learn in the past," I say regretfully.

"I want to be ready in season and out because there are so many who don't know You, but I have so much work to do! Lord, I am reaping the fruit of an undisciplined life, and making excuses, 'It's too hard!' Your Word says that 'I can do all things through Christ who strengthens me' and that I have the 'mind of Christ'! Moreover, You say I am a partaker of Your divine nature!"

The tension in me is so real! (Philippians 4:13; Philippians 2:5-8; 2 Peter 1:3-4.)

"Now, you are getting it, My love," You say. "The Bride gets herself ready by cleansing first, through the washing of the water of the Word." (Ephesians 5:26)

"Then oils. Let My Spirit soak into all the dry places."

"I AM THE BREAD FROM HEAVEN; THE BREAD OF LIFE. IF ANYONE EATS THIS BREAD, HE WILL LIVE FOREVER. WHOEVER EATS MY FLESH AND DRINKS MY BLOOD REMAINS IN ME AND I IN HIM. THE ONE WHO FEEDS ON ME WILL LIVE BECAUSE OF ME." (JOHN 6:51 NASB)

You remind me that your "food" is to do the will of the Father. There are many avenues for me to find Your will: Pray in the Spirit; commune with God; make declarations; worship and praise, adoration.

"Focus on Me," You say. "'I only do what I see My Father doing' (John 5:19). Don't forget that I have told you that you can do likewise."

"Lord, I want to dwell in the secret place of the Most High." (Psalm 91)

"Remember, your words matter, My love. 'Life and death are in the power of the tongue' (Proverbs 18:21). Speak what I have said about you. If you cannot remember at times, feast on My Word. I have only spoken Life over you."

IT'S YOUR TURN TO PRACTICE

This week, try taking communion each day, purposefully dedicating each day to Him. Take time at the end of the day to express gratitude to Him for what happened during the day. Worship Him throughout the day.

The following are sample questions to ask.

1. Where in my life have I had some confusion?

2. Have I been hiding the Word in my heart? Have I been in the habit of communing with Him?

3. Do I give Him thanks in your prayer time, or do I only tell Him your worries?

4. Am I getting clarity in an area that I didn't have before?

Be aware of how you speak this week. Are you saying what the Lord would say—about yourself, about others? (See the chapter called "Like a Rocket" and the comments in the section titled "It's Your Turn to Practice.")

Chapter 23

GREENHOUSE

I see myself standing outside a greenhouse, a place I've visited many times before. I'm wearing a white lace dress. I can see my arms—not as thin as I usually imagine myself.

You come to the door Yourself. You ask me, "Why do you wait outside? Don't you know that all that I have is yours? It is your inheritance in Me. I paid for everything. EVERYTHING. Come inside."

As I enter, my body feels suddenly energetic. The fragrances in this place are invigorating! "Oh Jesus, thank You!"

There are prisms of light dancing all around me, and the sunlight shines through the glass overhead. I see the Shasta daisies smiling and dancing. Hmm … *Shasta* means white; daisy means "day's eye"; it opens in the day and closes at night. It also means purely innocent, loyal love, beauty, patience, and simplicity. "Flowering mead." Selah.

I see You behind a counter. You hand me tickets to go anywhere. It's strange to me because I see You wispy, then 3-D, but at the same time, all over the place! You keep appearing as if to say, "Come and find Me!"

IF YOU SEEK ME, YOU WILL FIND ME, IF YOU SEEK ME WITH ALL OF YOUR HEART. (JEREMIAH 29:13 NIV)

"Come sit awhile under My shade tree, My love. There is a canopy over you on this swing. Let Me sing love songs to you as you sway back and forth. Peace, be still, My darling. I know you are troubled."

You are singing tenderly to me. I see plants entangling me, but not in a bad way. Just vines, trying to pull me in to become one with the garden. The plants are singing. "You are the Vine, and I am the branch, Lord. As in John 15, I want to abide in You and bear much fruit."

There is sap in the vines, such sweetness! Honeysuckle? Trumpet vines?

"I want to be a voice for You, yet Your Voice is so faint to me." I am pining.

I see You taking petals in Your hands and rubbing them together, leaving a fine, sweet-smelling powder. You are rubbing it on my face.

"Lord, I want to look like You. I want to smell like You. I want people to see You when they see me."

"See the irises," You begin, "so many folds in the petals, so many varieties. They bring beauty year after year, withstanding harsh climates and multiplying in spite of it. Your life is like that. Beauty is coming from these trials. Out of the pain, there will be multiplication. You will see it, but it won't even be your effort. Just be, just grow here in My garden, and you will see an increase in your life effortlessly. I am the Vinedresser."

I am listening now to Misty Edward's song "The Heart is a Garden" from Mark 4. The seed is the Word; some fell on hard soil, wayside and then trampled, some on rocky ground that withered away, some among thorns that were choked out.

"Be careful how you hear," she sings," be careful how you listen."

The ones that fell on the fertile fallow ground, that which was carefully prepared and tilled, produced a harvest of thirty, sixty, and a hundredfold. Keep the Word and bear good fruit. Patience is the key.

---

*TO HIM WHO HAS, MORE WILL BE GIVEN. HE WHO
DOESN'T HAVE WILL HAVE IT TAKEN AWAY.
(MATTHEW 13:12 ESV)*

IT'S YOUR TURN TO PRACTICE

Spend time with God in the secret place. "Come away with Me, My love," He is calling to you (Song of Solomon 2:13). Talk to Him about your cares and concerns. Ask Him to take you away to His garden of refuge.

ARISE, COME, MY DARLING, MY BEAUTIFUL ONE, COME WITH ME. MY DOVE IN THE CLEFTS OF THE ROCK, IN THE HIDING PLACES ON THE MOUNTAINSIDE, SHOW ME YOUR FACE, LET ME HEAR YOUR VOICE; FOR YOUR VOICE IS SWEET, AND YOUR FACE IS LOVELY."
(SONG OF SONGS 2:13-14 NIV)

---

1. What do you see? What do you feel? Embrace His peace and let Him minister to those areas that are in pain.
2. Write out your dialogue with Him regarding your need. Allow Him to have your thoughts, take every thought captive (2 Corinthians 10:5). Don't argue. Yield to Him your emotions and allow Him to give you His perspective.
3. Meditate on the Scriptures spoken about in this chapter. Picture yourself in this scene or ask the Lord to take you into a scene from the Bible, particularly the love story between Him and you in Song of Songs.

    a. Where are you?

    b. What do you see Him doing?

    c. What do you perceive that He is beckoning for you to do?

Chapter 24

EXPANSION OF THE GARDEN

The One my soul loves is speaking to me:
"See, My beautiful one, I have not neglected the garden. On the outside, it appears to be overgrown with briars and thorny vines, making you believe there was no entry. However, I have been here inside all along, working and cultivating and nourishing living things. I have been preparing them for you, My love. My Dove, look at Me with dove's eyes.

"Come inside. See the beauty I have kept for you. Don't worry about the time that has passed. I am so glad you are here now. You have permission to come inside and stay for as long as you like. This is Our beautiful, intimate place and you won't believe how I have expanded it for you!

"It's a real place. It's really for you! You can sit and stay with Me, and you can invite friends to certain parts—not every area, however. When they come, they will find their secret labyrinth with Me."

"Lord, it's been so long. I didn't know if I would ever connect with You here again," I lament.

You reply, "When you came to Me before in this secret place, it was beautiful, and we enjoyed each other's fellowship. Unfortunately, that joy ended when those religious ideas crept in.

"Oh, child!" You say excitedly, "since you are back, I have so much to show you! Every petal, every leaf. How to cultivate, how to water, how to fertilize, how to breathe in the intoxicating fragrances.

"Explore with Me! We are going on a fantastic journey! Don't be afraid. I will be with you, and you don't have to strive.

"Some days, you will be able to grow things quickly. Other days, you will need to rest in knowing that I will reveal things over time. I have so much to show you in My garden! In My greenhouse. You will do well to sit and study and gaze on Me in this place. I will even show you secrets of how to unlock disabilities, sicknesses, and suffering. Here. In this place. I will give you dreams as well. Get your pen ready. Some things are for natural growth and health, and all the things I show you are for spiritual understanding."

I heard the word "calamus," so I looked it up on a variety of websites. It is a rattan palm, a leaf-climber with slender, reedy stems. It can grow up to two hundred meters tall. [Wow!] It grows with "wet feet"; a "water weed" found on edges of ponds, lakes, rivers.

It is also called "Sweet Flag," and is very fragrant. If collecting the plant, be aware that it will taste like the water it has been soaking in. Calamus is also known as a "bitter root" and works to aid in the expulsion of the digestive tract. Bitterroot excels in addressing throat colds, sore throats, irritable coughs, chest colds, and head colds. It is also an effective antihistamine due to aromatic oils. It is antimicrobial. Chewing this root works against poison, the plague, and all contagious diseases. It helps with head colds, reproductive issues, and libido. It increases the range for singing, increases energy, and allays hunger.

It is useful for headaches and anxiety.

OK Lord, what are You trying to tell me through this plant? What spiritual understanding can I apply to my life?

Lord, I, too, can grow almost endlessly like this plant, as I reside and soak along the edge of your waters (anointing). My life will take on a heavenly taste as I abide in You. The plant works to expel waste, just as I will help others get free of their baggage. The healing byproduct anointing on my life will heal those infected with poisons, the plague, and all contagious diseases, including issues in the reproductive system, and those that hinder the libido. I will have new zeal (increased energy). The song of my life will reach a broader range of people and will satisfy their hunger and thirst. Finally, the anointing will allow me to cast out the spirit of fear.

I say, "That is an incredible word Lord! I had no idea I could receive a prophecy through a plant name! Let it be as You have indicated. I am overwhelmed by Your goodness. What a difference one revelation makes. I want to teach on this."

HER DESERTS WILL BLOSSOM LIKE EDEN, HER BARREN WILDERNESS LIKE THE GARDEN OF THE LORD. JOY AND GLADNESS WILL BE FOUND IN HER, THANKSGIVING AND THE SOUND OF SINGING. (ISAIAH 51:3 NLT)

You smile and say, "Now you're getting it, My Love Dove. Step into what I have intended for you to be."

"Oh Lord, there is such exhilaration in my spirit! I see a little bridge in front of the greenhouse!"

I couldn't stop laughing! "Oh God, you are so good!"

(For the reader: We were pastoring a church called The Bridge—God was saying the Bridge was only a small footbridge to where He wants to take us! It was excellent news for me at the time!)

I even want to start taking care of plants now that I have a vision for it. It's so exciting!

I see You clipping leaves from the trees in our backyard now. Your back is toward me as I come out from inside the greenhouse. You motion for me to come and sit on the retaining wall with You. You have different-shaped leaves in Your hand. As You open Your hand, You point out the intricacies of each.

I AM THE VINE; YOU ARE THE BRANCH. IF YOU REMAIN IN ME, AND I IN YOU, YOU WILL BEAR MUCH FRUIT. APART FROM ME YOU CAN DO NOTHING. (JOHN 15:5 NIV)

I lean into Your side. My heart cries, "Lord, encounter me. I have been faithless, but You are so faithful."

You place the leaves in my hand and move to put Your strong arms around me. My head is near Your heart. I can hear Your heart beating. It sounds like the waves of the ocean, coupled with the sounds of the night, and the rushing wind all at the same time!

You stroke my hair as we sit. You smell masculine but sweet. I rub the leaves together, and a new fragrance emerges.

There are some starlings (birds) that are eager to be in Your Presence. One hops up to You; You take it on Your finger and stroke its breast. It leans in with contentment.

LOOK AT THE BIRDS OF THE AIR, THEY DO NOT SOW OR REAP OR GATHER INTO BARNS, YET YOUR FATHER FEEDS THEM. ARE YOU NOT OF MORE VALUE THAN THESE? (MATTHEW 6:26 ESV)

"Lord, I'm pleased!" I exclaim, "I don't think I'm worried right now! I give my children and all of their cares over to You. Lord, Your eye is on the sparrow—and I know You watch over us! Right now, I want dove's eyes. I want to see only You!"

My feet are bare, and I move them through the grass.

"Lord, I'm hesitating. My feet need so much healing. I don't always know how to believe You for healing. Lord, help my unbelief! So many around us need Your touch—healing of body, soul, and spirit. I do, too, Lord. Even more, I need freedom. I want to hunger and thirst for You more than anything else!"

Right now, I want to learn how to stay in the glory. I hear in my spirit, "Lightning strikes the ground and brings minerals and nutrients to the soil."

AROUND YOUR THRONE ARE RAINBOWS AND FLASHES OF LIGHTNING, RUMBLES, AND PEALS OF THUNDER. (REVELATION 4:5 NIV)

IT'S YOUR TURN TO PRACTICE

Ask the Lord to take you to His garden to the secret place He promised for you. Can you picture it? What does it look like?

Pay attention to your senses of smell, touch, and hearing. What do you hear? Is there something to taste?

Ask Him to help you fully experience intricate details. Each sense has a message of its own. You will likely come back here many times.

Is there an assignment the Lord has for you that germinates in this place?

Chapter 25

I SET A PLACE FOR YOU

I am speaking this out loud to the Lord.
"I set a place for You this morning for breakfast, and on Christmas, for dinner. I want You, Lord. Nothing else can satisfy. I want dove's eyes for You. At the same time, I want to find out and become who I am ... I want to become love, like You. It seems impossible for my little life, my little corner of the earth, with my little timid voice and limited vision. However, YOU ARE CHRIST IN ME, the hope of glory! Change my perspective, O God!"

OPEN YOUR MOUTH WIDE, AND I WILL FILL IT.
(PSALM 81:1b NIV)

"Jesus, you are the Lily of the Valley, the Rose of Sharon, the Lion of Judah. You are so beautiful, an intoxicatingly fragrant One, so fierce and Holy. 'Kadosh.' Bright and Morning Star.

"Communion with You. Fellowship in Your death, burial, and resurrection. Take me past the outer court, into the holy place, past the brazen altar, Lord, I want to see Your face. Take me in by the blood of the Lamb. The Divine Exchange. ("Holy of Holies," Paul Wilbur.)

"Lord. What if I lived like this?"

I hear You say, "Hello, My Love Dove. Keep coming up. Keep coming in. You are on the road less traveled but, oh, the rewards in seeking. Don't give up. Don't be disheartened. Don't let up.

"Rise up! Rise up! Rise up! Rise up in the joy of your inheritance! It's always here waiting for you! Whatever you see, you can not only have, but you can be! How I love you! Beautiful and radiant one!"

I begin to question. "Lord, what if I only see dirt?"

He replies, "You can be the soil where seeds of greatness, seeds of righteousness, seeds of Truth, and seeds of Love are planted."

I repeat my doubt, "Lord, what if I only see a flower?"

He quickly responds, "I AM the Lily of the Valley and the Rose of Sharon. You can be a fragrant offering—an aroma of My goodness."

My heart begins to expand with possibilities. I continue the exchange with more excitement, "What if I see a building?"

His reply: "You can be a dwelling house for My Presence, a shelter from the storm, a strong tower for others to run into and be safe, a place to do My Father's business. In all these things, you are like Me. Which do you choose to be today?"

I think over my response carefully and say, "Let's start with the basics. I want to be dirt today. I am not motivated to do much work."

"But planting seeds is hard work, My dove," He replies lovingly. "Cultivating the soil is difficult."

"Oh yeah! I forgot!" I blurt out. "Thank You for teaching me today to cultivate the soil of my heart to receive Truth that prepares the ground for the fruit that comes forth."

Wisdom speaks again, "Cultivating is painful, My precious one. It uproots lies and deep roots that have been embedded for a long time. Often those roots are tangled up with other lies."

"Oh Lord, uproot lies in me! Lord, I want to be the good soil that Your seeds fall on and produce crops, thirty-, sixty- and a hundredfold!" I am resolute but timid.

Love continues, "You've only just had a taste of Me! Wait until I bring out all that I have for you. I am an overwhelming Flood, so be overwhelmed by My loving kindness …" (from a prophetic song by Kimberly and Alberto Rivera, *Wide Open*, 2014).

"I have exceedingly, abundantly above all that you have ever asked, dreamed, or imagined (Ephesians 3:20).

"I initiated it. You responded. Now I open up the floodgates for you. For you, My Love Dove. My queen."

"Oh Lord, even when I am faithless, You always remain faithful," I respond humbly.

IN YOUR PRESENCE, O GOD, THERE IS FULLNESS OF JOY. IN YOUR RIGHT HAND, THERE ARE PLEASURES EVERMORE. (PSALM 16:11 ESV)

IT'S YOUR TURN TO PRACTICE

Does God think the same way we think? In the above text, there is a stark contrast between how God thinks, and how I think (see Isaiah 55:8). Whenever we find this contrast and notice a gap, guess who needs to take action to change? The change process is wonderful, though, as we also get to catch glimpses of our true identity.

The following are simple exercises you can do to begin to change your perspective to match God's.

1. Picture "soil" or a building in your mind.
    a. What do you hear the Lord saying to you about it?
    b. What are Scriptures that talk about soil?
    c. What are the characteristics of the building? Meditate on these.

2. Picture a beautiful flower or find one outdoors. Look at the details.
    a. What is The Lord saying to you through the flower?
    b. The Lord may have you look up things in the natural to help you understand what He is trying to communicate.

Go a little deeper and ask the Lord how He sees you today. We have a precious prophetic friend, Marcy Benner, who told us a great exercise she learned for hearing God more clearly. Ask the Lord, "Do you love me?" When He says, "Yes" (He will never say "No" because He IS Love), pay attention to how that feels. This will be a plumb line, along with Scripture, for testing whether what you are hearing is from Him. If you are not hearing this clearly, there may be an area of your heart that needs to be healed. (Stay tuned for our next book, which will address some of these issues.)

Try setting a physical place for the Lord next to you in your home during dinner, during other activities, even watching TV. You may be surprised how He shows up!

Chapter 26

LET'S DANCE

The Lord is admonishing me, "Come away, come away with Me, My love! (from Song of Songs 2:10)

"My dove, full focus, full attention on the One you love and the One who loves you!

"Put aside the elementary things, My darling, My lily.

"For I have so … much … more … for you. In you. Through you.

"Do not be anxious that I'm doing them in new ways, with new people, with new ways of seeing things than you ever thought or imagined. For I AM the Unlimited One. I know all; I see all; I give My all—to you."

"Wow, Lord," I respond. "Show me some of the glory and grand plans You have for me! Fill me up, Lord, with You, not my own opinions."

I see myself on the terrace of Tom's restaurant (see "Restaurant on a Hill–The Return"). I am wearing an elegant gown, but it looks like a giant, mummy-like bandage!

You come over to me, smiling. You embrace me and then take hold of a piece of the bandage which causes me to spin around and around. I see a teal glow on You. Now this color is on me, as the bandage transforms into a beautiful satin dress. I am wearing pearls and look a lot like Cinderella. The dress is glowing, even singing, because You touched it.

I see a man wearing sunglasses and a beard. He's dressed in a suit; his back is sideways to us. He's playing a strange-looking electronic harp.

You smile at me. Your awesome smile. I saw Your eyes twinkle. You bow and say, "May I have this dance?"

I can't stop staring at Your rugged, beautiful face. Now our clothes are becoming gold.

I am beaming with delight. Your smile is so warm and genuine, like You are enjoying this dance as much as I am. Selah.

I am leaning into Your chest, feeling at peace as we peer out over the sea. The waves are crashing, the sun is setting, and the colors are brilliant orange, pink, and red.

My husband, Tom, comes up onto the terrace and into the room wearing a tuxedo. You take his hand and put it into mine. Then You embrace us as we stand hand in hand. You kiss us both on our heads and then blow on us until my head feels warm, like liquid honey. I see You back away.

"Don't go ..." I say, trying to cling to You.

You whisper, "Overflow. Revelation for others must come out of the overflow."

I'm learning, finally, that most of Your revelations are faint.

IT'S YOUR TURN TO PRACTICE

Engage Jesus by first priming the pump with your imagination. Envision yourself at the open-Heaven restaurant, as described in previous chapters. Walk around and take in as much of the scene as possible. From a place of peace, invite the Holy Spirit to take over the scene.

The following are sample questions to ask when you engage the Lord.

"Lord, could You show me some of Your glory?"

"Teach me how revelation comes from overflow. What can I do to practically walk this out?"

Ask the Lord to walk, dance, run, or do something you enjoy. Describe how the scene changes, what new revelation do you have?

Ask the Lord to take you to somewhere new. Describe the scenes He shows you. What are you wearing? What questions do you have for Him? Is there anyone else the Lord wants to connect you with intimately?

Chapter 27

BOXES

I see several beautiful boxes with decorated lids.

"Are these things stored away for me, Lord?" I ask. One of the boxes is half open with shoes inside.

You reply, "I have treasures stored up for you, My Love. These treasures are both practical and extravagant. You are worth it to Me, My dove. Remember what I've told you, 'Eyes on Me, eyes on Me. Whatever you see, you can not only have, but you can be.'"

After further reflection on His words, I hear a still, small Voice say, "I am not going to define you tonight, my Love Dove. My heart is for you to have it ALL! My heart is for you to see it and grab hold of it, and especially to see Me and walk close to Me.

"I did only what I saw My Father do (see John 5:19). You can do the same; everything I have is yours. Everything I AM is yours, stay close. I desire that you be one with Me/The Father/My Spirit.

"It is a mystery, yes. However, you came from Me, so it is natural." (Selah!)

"I AM wisdom, I AM understanding, I AM your Counselor, I AM your strength in the battle for miracles. I AM your Creator, and nothing is too hard for Me, not losing weight, not your job, your ministry, not healing, not miracles, not mysteries ... NOTHING will be too difficult for you. I AM the Source of all knowledge, and I AM ready and willing to share!

The fear and awesome reverence of the Lord is the beginning of wisdom. When you hear My voice, don't turn away. Stay. Listen. Then keep on listening. Seek, look and keep on looking. My divine power has given you everything you need for life and godliness—through your knowledge of ME!"

"Eyes on Me, eyes on Me;

"Whatever you see;

"You can not only have;

"But you can be.

"Do you believe it, My darling?"

I see a disabled girl in a wheelchair with circular blue waves going around and around her legs. Now the waves are going around her arms as she lifts herself from the chair.

I see You helping her up. Your hair has blue light waves running through it; Your gaze is intense and focused.

You motion for me to come and put my hand on Your hand. A bolt of electricity shoots from her feet through her spine and head.

She stands straight up, weeping and praising and shaking. My hands pulsate with power and blue light like Yours. I co-labored with You, but I know You are telling me that I am to initiate.

IT'S YOUR TURN TO PRACTICE

Get alone with God and remove distractions. Spend time meditating on the various aspects of His character. For example, John Paul Jackson wrote in his book *I AM: 365 Names of God,* "God is good, He is our exceedingly great reward, Prince of Peace, Restorer of our soul, both the Giver and the Gift, Preparer of our place in Heaven, Friend of sinners, longsuffering, gracious, Forgiver of all transgressions, Manna coming down from Heaven, Bread of Life," etc.

Continue to meditate on His names and attributes. When one is highlighted to you, stop and ask Him a few questions.

1. "Lord, please show me a vision depicting how I can co-labor with You to reveal this aspect of Your character." (For example, I described above how I saw a picture of me co-laboring with Jesus for someone's healing.)

2. Then ask, "In what areas can I initiate action toward the fulfillment of this vision?"

   a. What are the various opportunities available?

   b. Are there any obstacles that impede progress?

   c. What are the creative ways around those obstacles?

In *The Passion Translation of the Song of Songs,* (Passion and Fire Ministries, 2018), a commentary on verse 1:2 states: "The word for *Shulamite* and the word for *Solomon* are taken from the same Hebrew root word; one is masculine, the other feminine. The name Solomon occurs seven times in this book, which points to the perfect King, Jesus Christ. We are one spirit with our King, united with Him. You have become the Shulamite."

Meditate on this truth and ask the Lord what it means. Do you believe that you can be like Him?

Chapter 28

THE WINDMILL

I see a modern-looking windmill turning slowly beneath a gray, overcast sky. It begins to pick up speed. Soon the clouds part, making way for long rays of sunlight to touch the earth. I notice a nearby house. This scene reminds me of my slow-moving life. I must turn to the wind of Your Spirit.

When we believe we are small, we don't prepare for the times of divine connection. However, praise God, as David Koz sings, "As long as you are breathing, you can start all over again!" His Word says His mercies are new EVERY morning! (Lamentations 3:23)

I see a deep-sea fisherman getting all geared up. There is much preparation initially, and there is clean-up afterward.

Acquiring the gear takes time, but once you have it, it's turn-key.

Preparation in the secret place. In the meditation of the Word. In the faith-cultivating garden.

"Lord," I inquire, "Remind me again, if You please. I want to 'get' this. I've missed opportunities because I did not prepare, and I did not prepare because of small thinking. Small thinking kept me from pressing into the dream You have for me. My scroll, the one written before the foundation of the earth" (Psalm 139:16-17).

BECAUSE OF YOUR UNFAILING LOVE, I CAN ENTER YOUR HOUSE. I WILL WORSHIP YOU IN YOUR TEMPLE WITH PROFOUND AWE. LEAD ME IN THE RIGHT PATH, O GOD, OR MY ENEMIES WILL CONQUER ME. MAKE YOUR WAY PLAIN FOR ME TO FOLLOW. (PSALM 5:7-8 NLT)

I see a swan preening. I looked up "preening" and found out there are many reasons that birds preen: to remove parasites, to make feathers more aerodynamic and aligned, and to become more attractive to a mate. Selah.

IT'S YOUR TURN TO PRACTICE

Sometimes we can severely limit ourselves by the way we see ourselves. As long as we see ourselves as small, we don't prepare for greatness. Jeff Wittmer, founder of Burning Bush Life Coaching and California Collaborative Ministries as well as staff teacher at Bethel Church in Redding, California, teaches seminars about Deficit-Based Thinking (DBT) versus Abundance-Based Thinking (ABT). He eloquently tells us that "ABT isn't just positive thinking ... but a very intentional way to create 'brilliant shifts' in perspective. A way of reframing reality."

Deficit-Based Thinking is set on what is missing, what is wrong, what is lacking, what is broken, what is not working, or what is not happening in our lives. ABT, conversely, is an intentional way to create brilliant shifts in your perspective, small shifts in the way we filter and interpret our reality. "It is more than just positive thinking," Jeff says. "It turns toward the resource of the Kingdom and a higher law." Further, Jeff teaches that "Life is rigged by divine favor ... how can we develop our thinking to align with unfolding destiny and the abundance of the Kingdom?" (For more information, you will want to go to www.burningbushlifecoaching.com.)

1. In what ways do we limit ourselves by small thinking?

2. Where have you seen yourself small?

3. What are ways you can shift your perspective toward God's vantage point?

Dare to dream big. What is the Lord showing you regarding a specific aspiration? As the Wittmers have taught us, if you had plenty of money, time, and you knew you couldn't fail, what would you do? What could you do now to take steps to make that dream a reality?

Do you need to do some preening to be ready for opportunities? Allow the Lord to guide your thoughts toward the abundance He has waiting for you.

Are there areas in your heart that need healing in order to get where you want to go? Ask the Lord to highlight issues that could be hindering your ability to receive all that He wants to give.

Chapter 29

LIKE A ROCKET

In another time of intense worship, I was pressing into the "Yod," the smallest part of the Presence of God. I saw eyes, the eyes of Wisdom. Then I saw all kinds of eyes from many, many different types of people and creatures.

I kept pressing in. I saw myself in outer space. My body physically started shaking, like you might see a rocket shake as it bursts into new atmospheres during space travel. I was then sitting on a ring of a planet looking out. The sky opened up. I asked my spirit to encompass my soul. I marveled as I saw it spiral around and around as we (my spirit and soul) moved toward the bright Light. *Lord, I need understanding!*

I saw a lake on a distant planet. As I drew closer, I noticed colors dancing across the water like the Northern Lights, the Aurora Borealis. The water was a deep, vibrant blue with shimmering "diamonds" on the surface. Massive boulders and jagged rocks lined the shoreline leading to an open cave. *Should I explore? Perhaps another time.*

The scene changed to another lake, not as beautiful as the first. With newfound authority, I commanded the body of water to recede and it obeyed. *Wow, that was fun!* The edge of the shoreline continued to retreat, leaving only deep caverns and monolithic rock formations. I attempted to reverse this command, but nothing changed.

Earlier that day, I had seen a vision of a great blue piece of fabric unfolding out of deep darkness while hearing a deep, melodic, groaning sound echoing throughout the cosmos. I then saw a massive flash of white light!

Then I was back in my chair at the conference. I wondered, *Did I get a glimpse of creation in motion?*

IT'S YOUR TURN TO PRACTICE

In this activation, I want you first to make a declaration. Say something like, "Father, I thank You for all You have provided for us in Christ Jesus. I don't want low living. I'm not going to be held back anymore! I want to be like Jesus. Holy Spirit, I give You permission to change my thinking and to change my actions and to empower me to do what You do. I declare Your Kingdom come; Your will be done in me as it is in Heaven."

Now, take it a step further and ask the Holy Spirit to show you where you are seated (see Ephesians 2:6). If there are any hindrances, please refer to and meditate on the Truth of the Scriptures I have laid out above. If you are not sure of your standing with Him, please refer to Appendix C.

Begin by seeing yourself seated with Him in Heavenly places. Let Him show you the joy of that place. Have an adventure with Him!

Then, from that place of authority, I want you to speak. What is the Lord showing you to declare Truth over?

Sample questions for the Lord using the scenes of this vision.

What is He having you declare over:
- Your dreams?
- Your health?
- Your loved ones?
- Your finances?
- Your church?
- Your leaders?
- Your state?
- Your country?

Chapter 30

THE KITCHEN

I see a large kitchen, like at a restaurant. I am observing from behind a post. I notice how clean the kitchen is, yet how busy. I am given eggs to whisk—an easy task. I am thrilled that I am allowed in the kitchen among all these expert chefs! I observe their tenacious focus as they create such artistic, yet delightful and nourishing, foods.

Every so often, each person stops and tunes in to listen to the Master Chef's instructions.

I stop to tune in … Cinnamon and nutmeg go into the egg mixture.

I wait. *It feels like such a long time.*

I marvel at the clean counters; only a few chefs have flour or other spills on their aprons. The experienced ones work seemingly effortlessly.

"Hello, My Love Dove," I hear You whisper. "I love you. I am single-minded, believe it or not, when I look at you. My intentions are always for your good. When we talk, I am never distracted, anxious, or in a hurry.

"I AM your Healer.

"I AM your Defender.

"I AM your Provider.

"I have access to everything you need."

IT'S YOUR TURN TO PRACTICE

Prepare your heart by removing distractions. Begin by thanking the Lord that you have access, not by your merit, but by the precious and powerful blood of Jesus!

These are some questions you could ask the Lord about becoming more in tune with His instructions.

1. Lord, please remind me of a time when I heard Your voice and acted on Your word, resulting in a positive outcome. Please help me understand why it worked so well.

2. Conversely, remind me of a time that I did not recognize Your voice. What could I do better next time?

3. What are some ways I can share Your word with others?

4. What word of encouragement could I give to a friend this week?

Chapter 31

THE CLIMB

I see myself hanging off a cliff by one hand. Eventually, I swing my second hand up to hold myself. I am wearing gloves that help me grip; at least I was somewhat prepared. I see my arms are strong; my body is svelte. I don't remember seeing myself like this before. I'm wearing shorts and a cute T-shirt, a harness, rock-climbing shoes, and a chalk bag.

My husband Tom is up ahead, waiting to grab my hand. I know I will have to let go to take his hand. He has a firm stance and a firm grip. With his help, I quickly raise myself up from this precarious place. I should have taken another path, and it was not wise to be in that spot, but my muscles and my husband were ready to scale the wall even still.

How can that be, Lord? I think to myself. *In the natural, I am so heavy and weak. I am confident and strong in this vision.*

As Tom and I are standing on the side of the mountain, preparing to go up further (Tom is fully decked out in gear), I see blinding, blinking headlights from down below directed at us, trying to make us fall. I even hear honking noises—so obnoxious in this natural, serene landscape.

It is the enemy trying to bring us down, discouraging us from completing our mission. We realize that the lights and the noise cannot touch us way up here. The farther up we go, the fainter the sounds and sights will be.

Tom asks me if I want to go further. I admit that my muscles are a little shaky from the last ascent, but I am not fond of the noise or flashing lights. "Let's keep going," I suggest.

We walk around a flat place and realize that the air is cleaner and fresher. As we increase in altitude, we anticipate that it will be harder to breathe, but surprisingly it's not. It's invigorating, even intoxicating. We have a strong desire for more.

The sky is so blue, and the clouds have taken on different shapes. I notice one is a stallion with nostrils flaring. There are other horses, too. The horse clouds have nostrils flaring and are even pawing the ground. I say to them, "Go!" and they gallop down toward the annoying sounds. I hear a clash, even shofars, amid the commotion. Then silence as the horses float back into the sky, smiling and prancing.

Was this an angelic encounter?

IT'S YOUR TURN TO PRACTICE

Re-engage this encounter and allow the Lord to lead you to a higher place. Allow the Lord to take over the scene.

The following are a few questions you can ask along the way.

1. Is there an area of my life in which I'm trying to make an ascent, but the enemy is clamoring with all kinds of noise? How can I rise above it?

2. What are unique challenges you find as you're trusting Him to ascend? Are you discouraged by the disparaging words?

3. Try to shift your focus to the goal in mind. Try to change your gaze to the One who is calling you upward. What is He telling you?

Chapter 32

THE CRYSTAL HEART

I see a moving staircase. My steps upward are being accelerated, through no effort of my own! Roses and yellow daffodils line the stairs.

"Keep pressing in," You say.

"I am sorry I haven't been a good neighbor," I sheepishly reply, feeling conviction.

"Focus on Me, love," You patiently respond.

The stairs are becoming more of a moving walkway, but still going up. I am feeling a little uneasy, as it is very steep.

You are at the top of the escalator, motioning me to come up. You will catch me. I will not fall back.

I make it; I feel Your embrace, so loving, as my feet come off the floor.

"Lord, Your muscles are enormous! I know You don't really look like that, but I believe You are revealing some things about Your nature."

"You are getting it, My love," You respond, Your eyes full of fondness toward me. I could melt into the floor when you look at me like that.

I say, "Dove's eyes. Lord, I want to have dove's eyes toward You."

I see You holding something in Your hands. It looks like a crystal stone, but it has veins in it. The veins are pumping blood.

"I remove a heart of stone and give you a heart of flesh, My love," (Ezekiel 36:26) You say to me. "Flesh that can respond to My subtle leadings. The crystal looks good and is very important to reflect what is around it, but it hinders movement."

I see the crystal melting away as You simply gaze on it. You smile as You hold the beating heart in Your hand. You breathe on it. It begins to glow. You blow some more, and a flame starts to erupt. You gently place it into my chest. It hurts at first. I don't know if I can take the pain, but with every breath, with every beat, it starts to meld with my body.

131

"I want you to bake bread for others, My Love Dove."

How can I say no to You when You speak to me so kindly? I wonder.

"Figuratively, or practically, Lord?" I ask as I imagine a burnt loaf in the oven.

"Let's start with practically. Healthy bread. Find a recipe. I will help you. Then ask Me who to give it to," You direct me.

"I thought I shouldn't eat bread, Lord."

"That's not the assignment, and are you sure I said that? Will you obey Me, My love?"

"Can I get a bread machine?" I ask.

"Start with what you have," You tell me. "This will be an exercise in learning to hear My voice. Ask Me who to give it to and what to say. Then pray for them while you work on each one."

"Wow, Lord. I wasn't expecting this, but how exciting! I may burn a few, but I like this journey!" I respond excitedly.

There is no striving.
There is no striving in Your love.
Freely You have given to us.
You have made us Yours, LORD.
You have made us daughters and sons;
This is Who You are:
This is what Your love has done.
You are everything my heart needs,
All You ask is I believe.
(Rita Springer, *Battles*, 2015)

IT'S YOUR TURN TO PRACTICE

Being in sync with the heartbeat of God often means we will be open to sharing with the lost. He was willing to leave the ninety-nine for just one lost sheep (see Luke 15). The trick is for us to do this without striving.

These are questions to guide your conversation with the Lord.

1. How can I naturally reach out to others in love, in peace, and without striving?

2. How can I posture my heart to hear Your subtle promptings?

3. Lord, who are You putting on my heart this week? (Is there something practical He is showing you to do for them? Press in to see; look and keep on looking.)

4. Is there a word of encouragement that He is telling you to share with them?

5. Write down any impressions you hear. You may think it is not noteworthy, but His impressions are often very faint. They have to be pursued or leaned into.

6. What are you going to do this week to bring this "love tap" from the Lord to that person?

Chapter 33

ANGELS TO THE RESCUE

ARE NOT ALL ANGELS MINISTERING SPIRITS SENT
TO SERVE THOSE WHO WILL INHERIT SALVATION?
(HEBREWS 1:14 NIV)

Have you ever thought about angels and their impact in your life? I have always believed in them and knew from Scripture that they were real, but I didn't really understand, and I am actually still a novice at seeing how they are constantly interacting with our lives. Most of the time, we think of them as being sent by God for our protection. I have some fun experiences that I want to share with you about that, but I must assure you, this is only scratching the surface.

After graduating from college in 1985, my first job as a speech therapist was on a Navajo reservation in northern New Mexico. I drove many, many miles over the rough, unpaved wilderness in a government-issue Chevy Blazer.

Late one night, I was driving back from a training in Gallup to my home in Farmington. There were very few cars on the dark highway. It was around 9:00 p.m. as I neared the tiny town of Crownpoint, which was the base for the Bureau of Indian Affairs, where I worked. That particular night was very dark. I could see the magnificent starry host, but no moon.

As I made my way down the ribbon of road, my headlights started to flicker. Off … on. Off … It might have been the alternator, and I was concerned. There are legends of strange spiritual occurrences in that area. This was, after all, the "badlands of New Mexico."

As I crested the hill in the darkness, doing the speed limit of fifty-five miles per hour, I realized there was an entire herd of horses standing in the road! There was no time to veer around them or do anything! I closed my eyes and said, "Oh dear God!" as I braced for impact, clutching the steering wheel tightly.

When I opened my eyes, I looked in the rearview mirror. The horses were precisely where they had been, undisturbed! I was on the other side of them with my lights back on brighter than ever! *Whoa! What is going on?! Was there a time warp? Was I just transported?!* My thoughts raced. I didn't have a grid for what I'd just experienced.

I drove the rest of the way home without difficulty. My parents marveled when I told them what had happened. The next day, my Blazer was not working. The mechanic stated that the timing belt was not only broken, but it was torn to shreds! He said it looked like I had been driving without it!

Not long afterward, I was listening to a sermon by John MacArthur on the radio on that same road. I was undone by the message of salvation, and for the first time gave my life to the Lordship of Jesus. I had been in church all my life, but I only knew Him as Savior; I didn't realize that surrender was where the transformation begins.

The Lord really looked after me in the years I worked on that reservation. I was a young woman in my early twenties at the time, and we had no cell phones. I am sure I should have been afraid several times, but He really protected me.

On a cold, rainy day in March, I had been at a meeting in Crownpoint and was driving back to my home base at Dzilth Na O Dith Hle, near Bloomfield. The mud was very slippery, and even though I had the Blazer in four-wheel drive, I was not able to avoid slipping into a huge ditch—and then the Blazer rolled over onto its left side. I was wearing my seatbelt—and a dress. I remember thinking, *Now what?* and dreading what it could look like trying to get out of this mess. *Would the CB radio work?* I wondered.

Sometimes it didn't. I was at least twenty miles from the main road, and who knows how far from a home where anyone spoke English—or any home at all, for that matter. Not to mention that it was so muddy!

As I sat there, sideways, with these thoughts running through my head, the Blazer suddenly lifted up back onto its wheels and back onto the road! I put it in drive, and off I went without even a hiccup!

I don't think I realized at the time that I had just encountered an angel. I don't think I thanked him, either!

On another occasion, I was driving from Magdelena on a hot June afternoon to meet up with friends in Cañoncito who would carpool back to Albuquerque, where I lived at the time. I was driving a government-issue car without a car phone (and there were no cell phones at that time), going too fast around a curve on a "washboard" surface. My car spun out, and I ended up on the side of the road. Thanks be to God I was not injured, but one of the wheels was bent, and one had actually come off!

"Oh my!"

I had a habit of bringing a small daypack with water and a snack everywhere I went. I got out of the car, strapped on the pack, and started walking. It was hot and dry and the road was very long, very dusty, and very lonely. I hardly ever saw anyone on it. I wondered how long it would take to find a ranch so I could ask for help.

I had walked maybe ten feet when a water truck started coming down the road. This was unusual. Even more extraordinary was that there were two very tall Native American men with glowing skin and big, bright smiles driving it. The Navajo men I was accustomed to were typically shorter than these men were, and generally a bit more subdued around me as well. Because of their culture, they did not look you in the eye. But these men had smiling eyes that pierced my soul, and infectious joy.

They got out and started to work. They had just the right equipment to air the tires and pull the car back up onto the road with a winch. I marveled at how happy they seemed, and how friendly.

"This car will get you fifty miles," the driver told me as they were finishing up. My new friends climbed back into their truck; I watched in amazement as they disappeared down the road. If you are wondering, they did not "vanish"; I saw them go. I also carefully watched the odometer as I drove back to Cañoncito, which was exactly fifty miles. I was able to meet my carpool just in time. And when I parked the car, it actually fell apart! It had to be towed the next day. The axle was broken from my accident!

I was getting wiser by this time as I realized, "Those were angels! Wow! Thank You, Lord Jesus! Your eye is on the sparrow, and I know You watch over me!"

Angels can also be encountered in dreams. Tom has had some powerful encounters with angels in dreams. If we look at Scripture, there are a lot of examples of revelation and angelic encounter occurring in dreams. In fact, our friend Sandie Freed stated in her book *Dream On: Unlocking Your Dreams and Visions* (Sandie Freed, 2002) that she was feeling as if angelic experiences in dreams were not as important as face-to-face encounters. She wrote that the Lord rebuked her by saying, "Well, if it was good enough to save My only

Son, a dream with an angel is good enough for you!" (See Matthew 2:13-23, which tells of Joseph's dream warning him to take Mary and escape to Egypt so that Jesus would not be killed by Herod!)

Angels are known for protecting us, as demonstrated by the encounters I have described. They are also called "ministering spirits" (Hebrews 1:14). I have sometimes audibly heard their voices during worship. I have felt their presence many times in several different settings, but I have most often sensed them during corporate worship. I could feel their weighty presence so much that sometimes I could hardly stand. There was confirmation that what I was experiencing were angels when others reported similar impressions and still others explained their visions of these angels.

Angels are ministering spirits sent to partner with us as we do the Lord's bidding. As an example, one day while I was serving on a healing team at Bethel Church in Redding, California, I saw with my spiritual eyes an angel walking across the room delivering a liver on a silver platter. It was very brief and very faint. I wasn't even sure I should share it with my team, wondering if I might have gotten it wrong. However, I have learned this is often how the Lord speaks, so I shared the experience.

Right after that, a missionary came to our team and told us she had been diagnosed with a liver condition. We prayed in faith in recognition that the Lord was answering her prayer through the angel. She was overcome with the power of God and we all rejoiced with her as she received her miracle.

Tom and I were pastoring a church in Dallas when I read a fantastic book by Gary Oates called *Open My Eyes, Lord* (Open Heaven Publications, 2004). In it, Gary chronicles his spiritual journey, from not having supernatural encounters to later having them all the time. We wanted that for our church.

I was delighted to learn the author was hosting a conference in Moravian Falls, North Carolina. I remembered many prophets had reported having angelic encounters there due to the hundred years of prayer from the early Moravian Pilgrims. I easily convinced my husband that we needed to go.

The conference did not disappoint. Tom was having angelic visions, and others from our church reported amazing things as well. Gary Oates, Larry Randolph, and Bonnie Jones had led us into "deep waters."

After the conference ended, our group decided to play games in our beautiful, peaceful cabin, but I went for a walk up to Prayer Mountain alone. I didn't receive a lot of noteworthy revelation there, and I was a little disappointed.

As I headed back to our cabin, I began to hear something. It was one of the most incredible sounds I had ever heard: shofars were ringing throughout the valley! Over and over they trumpeted in harmony. It sounded like hundreds of them. They played for what seemed like a long time—so majestic and so electrifying! I wish I had stopped to inquire of the Lord about them. It was a truly holy moment. Instead, I was so excited, I began running up the hill to go tell the others. I breathlessly shouted as I reached the porch, "Come and see! Come and see!"

They all scrambled and started running down after me. Unfortunately, by the time we got there, it was over. I have asked the Lord many times what that was all about. I will let you know when I get an answer that is complete!

IT'S YOUR TURN TO PRACTICE

Just as we are learning to see with the eyes of our heart for vision, we can learn to see into the spirit for angels and angelic activity. Have you had an experience with an angel? If so, what was it like? Can you go deeper and ask the Lord to show you more about that encounter?

If you are not sure, begin to meditate on some Scriptures in the Bible regarding angels. Ask the Lord to help you to partner with the angels in ministry.

Ask the Lord to show you a vision of a time that an angel was present ministering to you, protecting you, or partnering with you.

Chapter 34

THE BRANDING

---

*AND I CONTINUALLY LONG TO KNOW THE
WONDERS OF JESUS MORE FULLY AND TO EXPERIENCE
THE OVERFLOWING POWER OF HIS RESURRECTION
WORKING IN ME. I WILL BE ONE WITH HIM IN HIS
SUFFERINGS AND I WILL BE ONE WITH HIM IN HIS
DEATH. (PHILIPPIANS 3:10 TPT)*

During a time of intense corporate worship, I reflected upon a recent Bible study on the Hebrew names of God. The name "Yod," is the smallest piece of Presence in the "Yod Hey Vav Hey," the Hebrew name of the I AM (Exodus 3:14; John 8:24). I was honoring the "Yod," thanking God for it, but I was asking for more of the "Hey," which means "the revealing."

It didn't take long before I had a vision. I was standing on the edge of a beautiful sea. There were different hues of brown on a sandy beach, which melted into white caps on the sea, then gradients of green, then shades of deep blue.

I pressed further in; I looked, waited, and kept on looking (Revelation, Daniel). I was now in the "Hey"—" the door to the place of awe and wonder, the place of "the Breath of God."

I saw an altar of fire on top of the water; a consuming fire now enveloped the entire scene. I intuitively knew to put my hands into the fire, but I was hesitant. I obeyed the prompting; it was not as hot as I expected. I watched as brands were etched into each hand, first, the symbol of "Hey" on the right palm. I knew a little of what this symbol meant, but there was another symbol I did not recognize etched onto my left hand.

The words "Belonging to the Lord" (from Isaiah 44:5) appeared etched into my right arm.

Then suddenly, I was back in corporate worship. I felt to place my right hand on my heart, asking for more and more of the "Hey" (to be etched there), and then I set my left hand on my head.

After worship, I looked up the meaning of the symbol on my left hand. It was "La-med," which is the symbol for "learning," as well as "authority" (shaped like a shepherd's staff); it can also mean "the heart (or house) that is taught". "Hey" on my right palm means "the door" or "the revealing." *Oh God, I want to know Your secrets!!*

The Hebrew alphabet is referred to as the "living letters," as they speak volumes of meaning in a single "jot or tittle." (Matthew 5:18 states "till Heaven and earth pass, not one jot or tittle will pass away from the law until all be fulfilled.")

Have you ever considered this? The Lord spoke the worlds into existence. Likely, He used the language of Heaven, the *living* letters. At the same time, 2 Corinthians 3:3 states we are "*living letters* ... written not with ink, but the Spirit of the living God, not on tablets of stone, but on tablets of human hearts."

There was a reverential fear of the Lord as I had this encounter. "God is Light, and in Him, there is no darkness" (1 John 1:5). Holy fire is in His eyes. He calls us higher. "If we claim to have fellowship with Him yet walk in the darkness, we lie and deceive ourselves" (1 John 1:6). Let His cleansing gaze reveal what needs attention. Be honest about it and ask for forgiveness. His perfect sacrifice was very costly to make way for your communion with Him.

IT'S YOUR TURN TO PRACTICE

Present yourself to the Lord in worship. Ask God to show you the *living* letters personalized for you. Gaze upon Him and keep looking. Start with the "Yod" of God, *the smallest piece of His Presence.* Ask Him for the "Hey", *the door to the place of awe and wonder, the place of the Breath of God.* Write about what you see and experience.

Sample questions for the Lord using the scenes of this vision.

1. What Hebrew symbols would You like to highlight for me?

2. How can I experience more of Your awe and wonder?

3. Would You like me to research Hebrew names and attributes of God?

4. In Proverbs 25:2, You say that it is, "the glory of God to conceal a matter and the glory of kings to search it out" (Proverbs 25:2).

   a. What are the benefits of searching for that which is hidden?

   b. In what ways is this like an Easter egg hunt for children?

Chapter 35

THE BUBBLE

I SAW IN THE RIGHT HAND OF HIM WHO SAT ON THE THRONE A BOOK WRITTEN INSIDE AND ON THE BACK, SEALED UP WITH SEVEN SEALS. AND I SAW A STRONG ANGEL PROCLAIMING WITH A LOUD VOICE, "WHO IS WORTHY TO OPEN THE BOOK AND TO BREAK ITS SEALS?" AND NO ONE IN HEAVEN OR IN THE EARTH WAS ABLE TO OPEN THE BOOK OR TO LOOK INTO IT. THEN I BEGAN TO WEEP GREATLY BECAUSE NO ONE WAS FOUND WORTHY TO OPEN THE BOOK OR TO LOOK INTO IT. AND ONE OF THE ELDERS SAID TO ME, "STOP WEEPING; BEHOLD, THE LION THAT IS FROM THE TRIBE OF JUDAH, THE ROOT OF DAVID, HAS OVERCOME SO AS TO OPEN THE BOOK AND ITS SEVEN SEALS."
(REVELATION 5: 1-5 NASB)

Lord, I see a bubble. I am inside it, floating above the city. I am pressing my hands and face into the sides. I marvel that it does not pop. Instead, it is stretchy and bouncy.

We are floating over a city; it is an ancient city, yet well maintained and beautiful. The early morning sun is reflecting off the walls and rooftops of the buildings.

An old woman is bringing out a sign to put in front of her shop. She is stooped over as if in pain, but she moves about the space with the familiarity of many years. She pats her dark, silver-streaked hair to make sure her bun is in place. She smiles and closes her eyes as she looks toward the sun. As she opens her eyelids, they reveal a magnificent shade of deep blue—almost crystal clear.

She is accustomed to seeing in another realm. I move in closer (still inside the bubble). She smiles broadly and says, "Good morning!" She is obviously used to seeing unusual things.

I start to wave, but it upsets my equilibrium, and my bubble starts moving around and around. I am dismayed and concerned about getting sick, but the old woman just laughs and says, "Come here." My bubble floats to the sidewalk below. The woman touches it, and it pops—leaving me sitting in a puddle of sticky wetness.

"Good morning!" she says again. I smile and chuckle as she extends her hand to help me up. She may look feeble, but this woman is actually powerful. "I've been expecting you," she adds.

I am wary as I know to test the spirits to see whether they are from God (1 John 4:1). This is my first encounter with someone in the spirit realm that is not clearly the Lord or one of His angels. (We should still test angels as well.)

"Where are we and who are you, please?" I inquire.

"It is good that you are asking. I am a fellow servant, like you, who has come in the name of our glorious Savior, Jesus Christ of Nazareth, the Son of God who shed His blood for the remission of sins. Where you are is not as important as why you are here. The Father has brought you here to receive an impartation for your next assignment."

Assignment? I ponder the word as she reads my thoughts.

"The Lord has created you for a purpose, Dove. Yes, I know His name for you. You are on a journey. You told Him you want all that is written on your scroll, correct?"

I nod, reflecting.

"That means there are assignments and adventures along the way," she tells me. "You can choose to accept them now or to shy away, even to ignore them, but they are necessary for intimacy, for oneness with Him—and with all of humanity."

IT'S YOUR TURN TO PRACTICE

Ask the Lord for a divine set-up with someone. Press into any impressions you may have. Look and keep on looking (as in Daniel, Ezekiel and Revelation). Things may not appear the way you thought they would.

Is there someone who is being sent to impart to you or to pray with you? Begin to ask the Lord to show you people you may never have thought would be in that role. Be sure that you test every spirit, every single time (1 John 4:1). Satan masquerades as an angel of light; he and his minions cannot proclaim that Jesus is the Messiah, the Lord and Savior of the world.

Ask Him to reveal things He has written on your scroll before the foundation of the earth. (See different translations of Scriptures above realizing that our DNA is also called a scroll or a "book". Selah!).

Are you willing to accept the assignments He has for you? Meditate on Philippians 3: 13-14. "… forgetting what is behind and straining toward what is ahead, I press on toward the goal to win the prize of God's heavenly calling in Christ Jesus!"

Chapter 36

A NEW INTERCESSION

I am meditating on this Scripture, and I see a precious one for whom I pray constantly. On this occasion, I see my friend on top of a very high, very steep, snow-capped mountain; this person is shivering and cold, with very little clothing.

I see myself go to her to bring a soft, heavy, warm blanket. She pushes me away, saying, "I'm fine." Yet her lips are blue and her body is shaking. I am warm and dry because I am dressed in white woolen clothing and proper footwear, gloves, and headgear. (See Galatians 3:27; Isaiah 61:10. "He has wrapped me in robes of righteousness...")

I call the angels, "Come, minister to my loved one, please." Suddenly, two huge angels appear and spread their wings out over us, shielding us from the bitter wind. They make a fire and spread leaves and logs for us to sit on. One even produces a cup of hot, creamy cocoa and hands it to the one I love sitting there. *Angels are so amazing! Thanks be to God!*

She reluctantly smiles as she sits and takes the cup. The angels are sitting with us. I am not sure whether she can see them, but the color is coming back to her face. This special one says, with a tremor in her voice, "I don't know how I got up here, and I sure don't know how I am going to get down!"

Revelation comes by peace, My love, I hear my Lord say. *Be at peace as you trust Me with those you love.*

"Would you like to get down?" I ask.

"Of course!" she says incredulously. "But it's too cold and steep!"

"I have some warm clothing for you, sweet friend," I offer as I think, *Lord, thank You for Your angels that shield her, even on this mountain of doubt and fear.*

"Are you warming up, friend?" I ask.

"A little," she says.

"Take this blanket, OK? I will sit next to you, and we will both be warm as we sit close together."

"OK, but don't put it on my feet. I don't like them to be confined."

"But your feet are purple!" I exclaim.

"I'm alright," comes the reply.

"At least put your feet by the fire," I urge. I see an angel blow on the embers since the fire has died down. It is now blazing. Warm and cozy.

"I love you," I say to my precious one.

"I love you, too," she says, laying her head against my shoulder.

I gaze out to my left. I see Jesus—or is it the Father? I see only His hands; His face is obscured by so much glory. He is inside a doorway in the sky with arms stretched out. So welcoming. So patient. So full of faith.

Outside the door, it is so cold, almost blizzard-like.

I can see a glimpse of something inside the door. His Essence is so warm and pure but inviting. I hear music and sounds of laughter in there.

My friend is leaning against me, wrapped in this safe, cozy blanket, sipping the special chocolate, seemingly unaware of the spectacular vision I am experiencing.

I am not cold, even in this environment. The angels are right here. I am not afraid. How could I be, knowing He is so close?

I trust You will never leave and that Your angels are faithful on their assignment, LORD, I say inside my heart.

The spirits of fear, anxiety, and doubt are shouting and taunting, but I can only hear a faint, muffled sound. It lets me know those spirits are not giving up, but shielded as we are, their voices mean nothing—like the tiny little nodlings in *Dragontales* who need a megaphone to be heard.

My loved one is safe and will always be safe from all attacks because I call for the angels and they are happy to minister to us. I open a window to the heavens for her.

Soon the fragrance and music and light and warmth of His Presence, of His goodness, will woo her into the safety of His Kingdom, and off the mountain of despair with which she has become so familiar.

"Fear, shame, offense, anxiety, sickness, rejection, and attacks of any kind, you ALL gotta go, in Jesus's name! Joy, faith, love, hope, acceptance, and peace are my loved one's portion forever!!" I begin to pray for my friend with all my heart.

Hmm … as I am sitting in this place with her, I see a dark blue cloth go into my ears to clean them out so that I can hear more clearly from His Spirit. After the cleansing, I hear the crashing of crystal waves from inside the doorway.

"Lord," I ask, "can I be bi-locational? Here, comforting and encouraging this friend whom I deeply love, and at the same time, entering into Your secret places?"

"YES!" is the emphatic reply.

So, I stay there with my loved one AND I walk up to the doorway, excited for what I am about to see. First, I turn to embrace my Lord to thank Him, but His arms and figure melt into the heavenly portal.

He says, "Come with Me, My love. I AM so close, but I love the game of hide and seek!"

I laugh as I step over the threshold into this captivating place. Water, water everywhere! Waterfalls are splashing all around me. I move from a frigid environment to a tropical one. No more need for winter clothing. With a thought, those garments disappear, and I am instantly wearing a gauzy white flowing jumpsuit with a blue sash. My hair is in a ponytail, and I sense I will not just be observing in this encounter!

A zip line appears, and I take hold of it. I fly through the air over the massive waterfalls cascading off the deep green monoliths. I am high up and moving so fast it takes my breath away. I am so excited and exhilarated as water splashes on me—so refreshing, but I am still dry!

Knowing my loved one is going to be OK frees me to experience the joy in this place. I see the Lord upon something that looks like a trapeze; He is doing aerial acrobatics up above me. It is fantastic! He then extends His hand and flings me up in the air, catching me one-handed on the way down!

Everything is so easy! So invigorating! I could stay in this place for eons! And maybe I will. I ask the Lord, "What made it so easy today? What made it different than other days of prayer when it's been hard to see You or feel You?"

"Focus. What you focus on, you empower, My Love Dove. If you focus on problems, you only see problems. You end up praying the problems.

Today, you concentrated on taking the solution to the one you love. My Kingdom is easy. My Kingdom is Light. My yoke is easy; My yoke is light." (See Matthew 11:28.)

"Eyes on Me; eyes on Me. Whatever you see, you can not only have, but you can be ..."

"My loved one is going to be OK," I declare to the Lord.

"Your loved one is definitely going to be OK," I hear Him say.

"Will You tell her that, LORD? In a way that she can hear?" I ask timidly.

"I AM, My love. I AM."

LOVE BEARS ALL THINGS, BELIEVES ALL THINGS, HOPES ALL THINGS, ENDURES ALL THINGS. LOVE NEVER FAILS. (1 CORINTHIANS 13:7-8 NIV)

On another day, I am asking the Lord to take me back to the mountain where I was with my friend, the one who resisted the offer to get out of the blizzard. We both have cocoa that never gets cold (thanks to the angels). Her bare feet are more pink than blue now as we sit by the fire.

"I love you," she says. I squeeze this one whom I love tightly and smile contentedly. *So grateful to You, Lord.*

I still see the portal out in front of us, beckoning. A whirl of color is coming out from it toward us; bubbles are being released. Tiny bubbles, medium bubbles, and huge bubbles are moving quietly but quickly toward us.

My precious one is leaning into my shoulder, oblivious to the glory bubbles landing on her. Her smile brightens and she starts to laugh a little. *Pop, pop, pop.* The bubbles land all around her, onto and into both of us!

I feel like dancing. She does, too. She begins to stand in her bare feet, then asks for some dancing slippers. The angels bring them to her. She and I hold hands and dance around the fire. Angels begin to join in, and they sing with a joyful rhythm. "Ho-ly; ho—leey; He is holy. Our Go-od."

The whirling colors start to move closer into all of us. As we dance, I feel almost intoxicated. My cherished one stops and says, "Do you see those lights?!"

"God, You are so faithful!" I whisper to You.

"I wonder where they lead?" she continues.

This is my intercession for my precious friend. So easy, and so peace-filled. Lord, You will carry her through. It will be amazing!

On another day, I pray, "I want to intercede for another friend now, LORD."

I see us at the top of another mountain—or is it the top of a canyon? We are looking out at the vast valley below. The future You have for him is on top of pillars throughout the canyon. One could expend a lot of effort getting there by going through each valley and climbing up, or by "faith walking" across (where there is no visible bridge).

"Hmm ..." I wonder, "how many times have I gone down into the valley, wandered around down there, and maybe even forgotten there was a place to ascend to?"

I want my precious friend to get across easily and quickly. Each word of encouragement I give seems to create a steppingstone, or a brick that starts to build a bridge to each pillar.

"Oh Lord, I speak to the bridge of encouragement to build his courage to move forward to find love, fulfilling employment, great relationships, financial freedom, astonishing health, divine encounters, and especially intimacy with You. Give me words of life for this one that I love!"

REMAIN IN ME, AND I WILL REMAIN IN YOU. FOR A BRANCH CANNOT PRODUCE FRUIT IF IT IS SEVERED FROM THE VINE, AND YOU CANNOT BEAR FRUIT UNLESS YOU REMAIN IN ME. (JOHN 15:4 NLT)

IT'S YOUR TURN TO PRACTICE

Think of someone you have interceded for many times without seeing results. Ask the Lord to take you into one of these scenes or a different one to help you gain a new vantage point for prayer.

The Scriptures say that Jesus only did what He saw the Father do (John 5:19). What is He doing in this scene? What is He saying?

Let the peace of God take over as you give this person into His loving hands. Remember to speak encouragement/life to this person in the natural as well. Speak to their potential rather than their limitations that are presenting themselves right now. That's what the Lord does with us through the prophetic word.

Chapter 37

IN HIS IMAGE

I am practicing seeing in the spirit in anticipation of my day. I see You at that place; Your arms are beckoning me to come to another dimension. I step into what looks like a portal to the left of us. You tell me to come up higher as You extend Your hand down to me through a wispy open cloud. You pull me through and now we are walking on top of that cloud.

It's mostly white, but hazy in this place. I see an angel at a desk typing. There is a heavy door made of a red wood. It has intricate, embossed designs of lilies and other flowers; I see ocean waves and tall trees engraved as well.

I knock on the door and the sound reverberates visibly. I hear, "What's the password?" I am thinking that it is going to be something very spiritual, and then I hear, "Sliced cheese!" and a giggle.

"OK, sliced cheese," I repeat.

The door automatically opens like a safe that just got unsealed. As it moves, I see small balls of light bouncing off the ground and spilling into the area where I am standing.

These orbs of light are piling up and beginning to pour over me. Soon, I am up to my neck in light bubbles.

"Lord, You are so much fun!" I exclaim. I begin to twist my body inside this envelopment. As I do, many of them pop and are absorbed into me, so much so that my body begins to disappear, with only my head visible.

The Lord asks if I trust Him. I do. I realize that I must dive all the way in—so I duck my head down and I am overtaken. I feel instantly lighter.

I look around. It feels as if I am looking through water, but it's not water. It's thicker. My movements are flowing and my hair billows with this liquid substance. It's becoming thicker, almost gooey.

"Let it permeate, My love," I sense You saying. "It is My liquid Love that I want you to marinate in. Even just a moment here will transform you. Let it saturate your body, your heart, your mind. Remember when I baptized you in this way years ago and filled you with My Spirit?"

Oh wow, Lord! That was the most powerful encounter of my life! My whole room literally glowed with amber light for hours while I felt Your intense Presence and learned to pray in the Spirit!

I taste something sweet like honey as it fills my mouth.

TASTE AND SEE THAT THE LORD IS GOOD. THOSE WHO FEAR HIM LACK NO GOOD THING. (PSALM 34:8 NASB)

This honey is so satisfying, like manna from Heaven.

I see this amber-colored liquid start to ooze into, not out of, my ears and eyes, even into my nostrils. You are heightening my senses. As it goes into my eyes, I see what looks like windshield wipers clearing off anything that would obscure my vision. Then it begins to swirl as if enabling me to see into unlimited dimensions.

I begin to smell a hint of cinnamon and I hear "cinnamon acacia" (a specific type of cinnamon). My sinuses are being cleared by this amazing, tangible, sticky substance. I breathe deeply, and as I do, the liquid seeps quickly into my lungs, my heart, my stomach. It feels like I am being scrubbed from the inside out. It's not painful, but I feel some discomfort as impurities are eliminated from my being.

My bloodstream is carrying this throughout my body. My tongue is being scrubbed so that my speech is sweet, like "apples of gold in settings of silver" (Proverbs 25:11). My teeth are being restored at the roots. From the place that words are uttered, a fountain of light explodes into my brain. As it cascades down, tiny candles of bright lights begin to create an organized grid that connects to my nervous system. Every neuron on every cell begins to spark, then illuminate. My toenails are now glowing. My fingers are emitting rays of light.

You come over to kiss me on the top of my head, and this incredible warm liquid quickly engulfs me. I am totally being transformed into Your image! I pick up my foot; I see rays of light. I move my hand and a wave of rainbow color becomes visible. I breathe deeply and a bright indigo powder goes into me, and then out of me, touching everything around me.

I say "Jesus" and swirls and swirls of colored light reverberate around me into the atmosphere. I touch the solid wall and it becomes light as I push my hand through it.

I say, "I love You," and the sound echoes with weighty Presence, moving into the atmosphere, permeating everything in its path. Wherever I walk and whatever I touch, the residue remains. I see swirls of color as I go outside in the natural and touch the plants outside. I say, "Life!" I feel Your tangible pleasure as I do this.

"Yes, love," I hear You whisper as You embrace me tightly, "Becoming love costs everything, but so much, so very much more is gained." You smile so warmly and affectionately. "As the Father has loved Me, so have I loved you. Remain in My love (John 15:9). Then, go and do likewise."

IT'S YOUR TURN TO PRACTICE

This was one of the most powerful encounters I've had in a very long time. I was greatly encouraged. I don't believe that I will ever be the same as I keep my gaze on Him.

It's your turn. Ask the Lord to envelope you with His amazing liquid Love. Allow His tangible Presence to become so real. Don't overthink it. Don't resist it. Just embrace it. There is nothing like His Love. (*"Where You Are,"* Leeland, 2018)

APPENDIX A
ONLINE PROPHETIC SCHOOL OFFER

We invite you to join our self-paced, online School of Prophetic Ministry (SPM). Allow the Holy Spirit to train you, equip you, and instill a new passion for intimacy with Jesus. As a byproduct, you will see an increase in your ability to hear and share messages from God. This course includes short instructional videos, prophetic activations, course manuals, quizzes, and homework. Your access will be available for life.

Use the link or QR code below to learn more and get a special book readers' discount on our website.

PropheticEquippers.com/school-of-prophetic-ministry-spm

APPENDIX B
IS THAT REALLY IN THE BIBLE?

Often people are concerned that visual imagery is not from the Bible. However, if we really take time to think about it, we will see that the Bible is chock full of stories of God communicating through vivid images, both in the Old Testament and the New.

Once, I (Marcia) was a part of leading a children's ministry in the public schools. The leaders instructed us emphatically that we were not to demonstrate "charismatic" doctrines or to use prophetic words. It was amusing to me, however, that on the first day that we observed this "mainline" Christian group, the leader stood up to tell the children about an elaborate picture she saw of a tree that had many branches and roots. I forgot the point of her lesson, but I smiled as I realized that often we are put off more by semantics than we are by principles. The enemy gains a lot of traction by trying to divide us with labels.

Jesus loved to use parables and metaphors. Saints of old saw open visions and dreamed dreams. There are no Scriptures that indicate that God no longer has the need or desire to speak to His children. He came so that we may have relationship with Him. It is amazing that we have the Word of God, and we can never, ever discount its importance to test everything, but remember Jesus is the Word of God made flesh Who still dwells among us (John 1:1). His desire is that we may know HIM and become one with Him (Philippians 3:10; John 17:21).

The following are just a few of the many examples found throughout Scripture.

"In the last days," God says, "I will pour out my Spirit on all people. Your sons and daughters will prophesy, your young men will see visions, your old men will dream dreams. Even on my servants, both men and women, I will pour out my Spirit in those days, and they will prophesy ..." (Joel 2:28)

Then the Lord took Abram outside and said to him, "Look up into the sky and count the stars if you can. That's how many descendants you will have!" (Genesis 15:5-6)

Joseph interpreted the dreams of Pharaoh and told his family about his own dreams. (Genesis 37-50)

"Don't be afraid," the prophet answered. "Those who are with us are more than those who are with them." Moreover, Elisha prayed, "Open his eyes, Lord, so that he may see." Then the Lord opened the servant's eyes, and he looked and saw the hills full of horses and chariots of fire all around Elisha." (2 Kings 6:16-17)

He commanded that we meditate (imagine/visualize) on His Word. (Joshua 1:8; 1 Chronicles 29:18)

"I saw a dream … and the visions in my mind …" (Daniel 4:5)

"I was looking in the visions in my mind; I was looking as I lay on my bed, and behold an angelic watcher, a holy one, descended from heaven." (Daniel 4:13)

"I will stand at my watch and station myself on the ramparts; I will look to see what he will say to me, and what answer I am to give to this complaint." (Habakkuk 2:1)

"I am the Door; if anyone enters through Me, he will be saved and will go in and out and find pasture." (John 10:9)

One thing I have asked of the LORD, that will I seek after, that I may dwell in the house of the LORD all the days of my life, to gaze upon the beauty of the LORD and to inquire in His temple. (Psalm 27: 4)

"Father, I want those You have given Me to be with Me where I am and to see My glory, the glory You have given Me because You loved Me before the creation of the world." (John 17:24)

"Ask, and it will be given to you; seek, and you will find; knock, and the door will be open to you. For everyone who asks receives, he who seeks finds, and to him who knocks, the door will be open to him." (Matthew 7: 7-8)

Jesus spoke to the crowd in parables; He did not say anything to them without using a parable. (Matthew 13:34)

He demonstrated that He ministered out of vision when He said in John 5:19 that He only did what He saw His Father do.

Peter saw a vision in Acts 11:4-9 in which the Lord showed him that he "should not call anything unclean that the Lord has made clean."

Paul was on the Damascus road when he saw a vision and heard the voice of Jesus (Acts 9). Ananias saw a vision that let him know it was safe for him to help Paul, this man who had severely persecuted the church, and he eventually prayed for him to be healed of blindness (Acts 9:11).

John was on the Isle of Patmos when he received the impartation for the entire book of Revelation.

For a more detailed account, check out Mark Virker's book "How to Hear God's Voice." Appendix B, *Rhema in the Bible*. Destiny Images, 2005.

APPENDIX C
FIRST THINGS FIRST

I wish I could tell you just how good the Gospel (the "good news") really is, but to be honest, I have to say I have only scratched the surface. You may have heard all kinds of things about the Christian life, but I am afraid that in the Church's zeal, we have often "called people out" on their sin, rather than "calling [them] up" to the higher life.

This life is in the one, true, living God, manifested in His Son, Yeshua, Jesus, who in His mercy, took all our sin, sickness, and death upon Himself. John 14:6 tells us Jesus said, "I AM the Way, the Truth, and the Life. No one comes to the Father but by Me. If you really know Me, you will know My Father as well."

GOD DEMONSTRATED HIS OWN LOVE FOR US IN THIS: WHILE WE WERE YET SINNERS, CHRIST DIED FOR US. (ROMANS 5:8 NIV)

HE HIMSELF BORE OUR SINS IN HIS BODY ON A TREE SO THAT WE MIGHT DIE TO SIN AND LIVE FOR RIGHTEOUSNESS. BY HIS WOUNDS, WE HAVE BEEN HEALED. (1 PETER 2:24 NIV)

His word says, "Be holy, as I AM holy" (1 Peter 1:15-16). This is an area where we often get stuck. We realize that we are not holy, and the more we try to become so, the more we see our shortcomings. We sometimes misunderstand the meaning of "holiness." Some scholars tell us the word actually means "transparency."

We don't understand what the word "sin" means, either. Sin means "to miss the mark"; it also has been defined as "a condition in which the heart is corrupted and inclined toward evil." Sin is the problem that corrupts the world and everything in it. We are powerless to truly overcome our sin apart from Jesus Christ.

How many times have we missed the mark of loving others when we became offended, refused to forgive, gossiped about, lusted after, or maligned a person created in the image of God? Read Matthew 5:22 if you want to know what Jesus said regarding speaking badly about one another! His goal in restoration is to bring to Himself all those made in His image. In Him, we are to be one.

We can try really hard to be "good," but how good is "good enough"? "God is Light, and in Him, there is NO darkness at all!" (1 John 1:5). I don't know anyone who's perfect, so when I compare myself to another person, I may feel pretty good—or really bad! How do we define "good"? Jesus told us that "only God is good" (Luke 18:19).

Isaiah 64:6 makes a rather shocking statement: "All of your RIGHTEOUSNESS is as filthy rags" to Him! You may notice He didn't say "your sins or mistakes"; He said, "righteous acts" by which you are trying to gain His favor. Only One obtained His favor. His name is Jesus Christ of Nazareth; Yeshua Ha Massiach, the Holy One of Israel!

Proverbs 29:18 tells us that "without a vision, My people cast off restraint." To me, that says if we don't know where God is taking us in life, then we won't have a vision for it and we will do whatever seems right at the time, as in "there is a way that seems right, but in the end, it leads to death" (Proverbs 14:12).

The Scripture tells us that sin has pleasure, for a time (see Hebrews 11:25), but it leaves a nasty aftertaste. He wants "to make known to us the path of life," and fill us with joy in His Presence, with "eternal pleasures at His right hand" (see Psalm 16:11). Do we want His path?

We find His path by confessing we've sinned and changing the way we think (the true meaning of "repentance"). The alternative is to deny that we need a Savior, thereby justifying ourselves in our own merit. Abstaining from this decision equates to denying a need for a Savior. I don't know about you, but I like having my sins blotted out. It sounds pretty good! Isaiah 1:18 says, "Though your sins were like scarlet, they shall be white as snow."

If you don't think this applies to you, Romans 3:23 states that "all have sinned and fallen short of the glory of God." Romans 6:23 tells us that "the wages of sin is death, but the gift of God is eternal life in Christ Jesus." Romans 5:9 further encourages us by stating, "Since we have now been justified by His blood, how much more will we be saved from God's wrath through Him?"

162

Friend, we don't get away with sin; it comes back to bite us. We see it all around us. Some people call it "karma," but this is a poor definition, actually. The Bible says it like this in Galatians 6:7-8: "Do not be deceived. God is not mocked. Whatever a man sows, that will he reap."

God made impersonal laws in His orderly universe. You will never "get away with" sin, there is always a price. People don't believe this because they don't see the repercussions instantly. For example, they cheat on their spouse and it seems that nothing happens—for a while. That's because justice turns slowly because of His mercy toward us. The worst consequence of all occurs if we hear God say, "Depart from me, for I never knew you" and we die (see Luke 13:27) without knowing His great love.

WHOEVER SOWS TO PLEASE THE FLESH, FROM THE FLESH WILL REAP DESTRUCTION; WHOEVER SOWS TO THE SPIRIT, FROM THE SPIRIT WILL REAP ETERNAL LIFE. (GALATIANS 6:8 NIV)

DON'T YOU KNOW THAT WHEN YOU OFFER YOURSELF TO SOMEONE AS OBEDIENT SLAVES, YOU ARE SLAVES TO THE ONE YOU OBEY—WHETHER YOU ARE SLAVES TO SIN, WHICH LEADS TO DEATH, OR TO OBEDIENCE, WHICH LEADS TO RIGHTEOUSNESS? (ROMANS 6:16 NIV)

The good news is that the Lord had a plan before the beginning of time to ensure that you would not be left out of the family. The Lord Himself took the penalty of sin, sickness, and death for all time for all people upon Himself! Real love is voluntary, though. He will not impose His will on you, but He has made it easy to turn to Him, and He is always lovingly inviting you to receive Him!

IF WE CLAIM TO BE WITHOUT SIN, WE DECEIVE OURSELVES, AND THE TRUTH IS NOT IN US. IF WE CONFESS OUR SINS, HE IS FAITHFUL AND JUST TO FORGIVE US OUR SINS AND TO CLEANSE US FROM ALL UNRIGHTEOUSNESS. IF WE CLAIM WE HAVE NOT SINNED, WE MAKE HIM OUT TO BE A LIAR, AND HIS WORD IS NOT IN US. (1 JOHN 1:8-9 NIV)

That, my friend, is where He so longingly desires you to be as well! He is seated at the right hand of the Father, and through His blood-drenched sacrifice, He made a way for you to be there, too!

Do you want to know who you REALLY are meant to be?! Ephesians 2:6 encourages us with incredible news! "And God raised us up with Christ and seated US WITH HIM in the heavenly realms in Christ Jesus, so that in the coming ages, He might show the incomparable riches of His grace, expressed in His kindness to us in Christ Jesus!"

It doesn't get any better than this!! Through our agreement with this blood covenant, which He made with Himself, He invites us to be "partakers of the Divine nature" (2 Peter 1:4). We can now begin to learn what it means to rule and reign and become One with Him (John 17:21) through the relationship we can begin developing.

Pray this prayer from your heart:

Lord Jesus, I have sinned. My sins have been wicked, ungodly, and against You. I turn from them and ask You to forgive me of all my sins. Blot out my transgressions and remove my shame. Make me clean and pure. I believe You can do this through the blood offered by Jesus on the cross. I believe Jesus not only died for me but also rose again on the third day, proving He was God. I now bow my heart to You and acknowledge Your leadership over my life. Help me grow into the man or woman You desire me to be. I thank You that I am now a believer. I am a Christian now and will be forever with You in Your Kingdom because of Your sacrifice for me. In Jesus's name, amen.

Now, take time to let the Lord minister to your heart regarding these things. He loves you with an everlasting love (Jeremiah 31:3).

Your life will never be the same!

BIOGRAPHY

Tom and Marcia Mawman founded the Bridge Church in Dallas, Texas, in 2011, and served as senior pastors for five years. They also founded the Prophetic Equippers School of Prophetic Ministry (SPM) in 2006, which has activated hundreds of people in the prophetic, and is still available and continually updated online.

Tom is a certified life coach and minister of inner healing and freedom. He has traveled with prophetic and deliverance ministry teams, bringing freedom to many in African and European nations. Tom serves on various prophetic teams at Bethel Church and as a team leader in the Healing Rooms.

Marcia is a speech pathologist and ordained minister, and partners with Tom in ministry. They have been married for twenty-seven years and live in beautiful Redding, California. Their two adult children, Jeremiah and Bethany, also have a prophetic bent and will soon move to Redding (hint hint) from their homes in Dallas, Texas.

On weekends, Tom and Marcia can be found jeeping, hiking, rock climbing, biking, or kayaking in the mountains around Redding with their friends and church family.

Made in the USA
Monee, IL
07 April 2022

94341292R00104